Learning the Guitar

for the

Music Therapist and Educator

by

Peter Joseph Zisa Ed.D., M.M.

Copyright 2017

Table of Contents

Preface vii
Introduction x
Music Therapy and Education x
   Guitars xiii
   Picking a Guitar xv
      Are All Guitars the Same? xv
      Does Size Matter? xvii
      Steel string or Nylon? xviii
   Parts of the Guitar xix
   Tuning Your Guitar xix
      Tuning Guitar to the Piano xx
      Relative Tuning xx
      Electronic Tuners xxi
      Recommendation for Ear Training xxii
   Guitar Maintenance xxiii
      Cleanliness xxiii
      Heat and Humidity xxiii
      When to Change Strings xxiv
Accessing the Videos xxiv
How is this method book different? xxv
Lesson 1: Acquiring the Know-How 1
   Holding the guitar 2
   Left hand exercises 3
   Exercise 1 3
   Exercise 2 3
   Exercise 3 4
   Improvisation Pieces 5
esson 2: Rhythm: the Dance of Time 7
   Meter 7
   Rhythm Notation 7
   Measures and Bar Lines 8
   Compose a Rhythm Song! 8
   Strumming: The Dance of the Right Hand 9

Two Chords	9
Exercise 1	9
Exercise 2	10
Exercise 3	10
Exercise 4	10
Arpeggio	11
Establish the Position	11
Pattern 1 and 2	12
Jacob's Ladder	12
Lesson 3: Music Notation	**14**
Rhythm and Note Types	14
Time Signatures	15
Meter and Time Signatures	15
Rhythm: The Dance of Time	16
Common Time: Quadruple Meter	16
Simple Quadruple Time and Strumming	16
Etude 1	16
Etude 1 ~ Rhythmic Strumming	17
Etude 2	17
Etude 2 ~ Rhythmic Strumming	18
Arpeggio	20
Establish the Foundation	20
Pattern 1 and 2	20
Prelude: Melodic Variety in Seventh Position	21
Jacob's Ladder	21
Lesson 4: Introducing Four Notes in First Position 1	**23**
16-Bar Blues in G	24
Two Chords: G7 and C	26
Strumming Rhythms Using Quarter, Half, and Whole Notes	26
Practice Strategy to Improve Chord Changes	27
Parallel Movement	27
Contrary Movement	28
C and G7 Chords with Simple Half-Note Strum	29
Using an Eighth-note Strum Pattern	29

    Three-Finger Arpeggio Pattern 30

    Chord Forms 30

    Wind Chimes 31

Lesson 5: Reading Notes in Position 1 33

    Five-line Notation and Treble (G) Clef 33

    Two New Chords: G and D 34

    Strumming a Syncopated Rhythm 35

    The Importance of Know How 36

    Reading Music Notation: Knowing What & When 36

    Scale Practice as a Warm-up 37

    Learning Your A, B, Cs 37

    Gold Fish & Syncopated Rhythms 38

Lesson 6: Filling in the Gaps 41

    Sight-Reading 42

    E-Z Does It 43

    Olé 44

    Arpeggio Pattern 1 and 2 45

    Preludio Del Amore 45

Lesson 7: Chords and Harmony 49

    Chords and Harmony 49

    Major and Minor chords 49

    Rhythm Guitar: Chords and Rhythm 50

    Chord Changes and Common Chord Tones 51

    Syncopated Rhythms 51

    Seventh Chords 51

    Two Songs to Learn 52

    Polyrhythmic Difficulties in Singing and Strumming 53

    Choosing the Complimentary Strum 53

    Scales and Melody 53

    G & A: Two Notes on the Third String 54

    Matching Melodic Tones with Chordal Harmony 55

    Varying and Expanding the Melodic Possibilities 55

Lesson 8: Shapes, Forms, & the Circle of Fifths 58

    Moving Sixths 58

- Am7 and Dm chords 58
- Am to Dm 59
- Am7 and E7 chords 59
- Harmonic Relationship of Using Scale Degrees 60
- The Circle of Fifths Relationship in Harmonic Progression 60
- Corresponding Arpeggiated Accompaniment 61
- G & A: Two Notes on the Third String 63
- Matching Melodic Tones with Chordal Harmony 63

Lesson 9: I - II7 - V7 Vamp 65
- C and D7 65
- D7 and G7 65
- Divide and Conquer 65
- Eight Notes on the First Three Strings 67
- Line Notes and Space Note 68

Lesson 10: Accidentals & Scaling the Fingerboard 72
- Accidentals 72
- Chromatic Scale 73
- Major Scale 74
- G Major Scale 75
- Bach in a Minuet: 75
- Practice strategy: 76
- Scales, Keys, and the Circle of Fifths 77
- Scale Practice 78
- Scale and Chord Practice 78
- The Written Notes of the Major Scale in Five Keys 79
- Ear-Training Challenge! 79

Lesson 11: Jazz Vamp: Dominant-Seventh Led Circle of Fifths 81
- Progression 1 81
- Progression 2 82
- Ragged Time 83
  - *Cakewalk Rhythm* 84

Lesson 12: Chord Summary & Harmonic Progressions & Transpositions 87
- I – V7; V7 – I Progression 87
- Transposition 87

    I - V7 Progression 88

    I-ii-V7-I Progression 89

    I-vi-ii-V7-I Progression 90

    The Capo and Harmonic Transposition 90

    Transposition Using Four Major Chord Shapes 91

Lesson 13: Open Bass Strings and Varied Arpeggios 93

    Open Bass Strings 93

    Notation of Open Bass Strings 93

    Prep for Etudes 1 & 2 94

    Etude 1 95

    Re-voiced Chord Forms 96

    Arpeggiated Variation 97

    Transposition Assignment 98

Lesson 14: Juggling: Combining Melody and Bass 100

    The Tune: A Simple Melodic Motif 100

    Adding the Bass 101

    The Coda 101

    Practice Strategy: 102

Lesson 15: Introduction to Spanish Flamenco & the Notes on String Four 105

    The Origins of Flamenco 105

    Flamenco Strumming 106

    Rasqueado Strum 106

    Notes on the Fourth String 107

    Phrygian Prelude 108

    Arpeggiated Flamenco Pattern 108

    Piazza Di Spagna 109

Lesson 16: Harps-Like Arpeggio Patterns in Triple Meter 113

    Block-chord forms versus Arpeggiated chord-form 113

    Notes on String Five 114

    Arpeggio Pattern in Triple Meter 116

    Traditional English Tune 117

    The Birth of Folk-Rock and the House of the Rising Sun 117

Lesson 17: Smokestack Lightening! 121

    The Notes on the Bass Strings 121

- Climbing the Ladder 121
- Climbing the Ladder 123
- Hop and Skip 123
- Bass String Etude: If you can say it, you can play it! 123
- How Do You Do? 124
- Iron Fly 125

Lesson 18: The Pentatonic Scale: A Scale for All Seasons and Times 127
- Pentatonic Scale 127
- Pentatonic Scale and Blues 127

Lesson 19: Tablature: Yesterday, Today, and… 132
- History of Guitar Notation 132

Lesson 20: Alternative Tunings 138
- Drop-D Tuning 138
- Jasmine 139
- DADGAD Tuning Its History and Use 141
- DADGAD Tuning 142

Summary Review 145

References 159

- About the Author ....**Error! Bookmark not defined.**

Preface

When I was 16 years old, my father encouraged me to take my guitar and visit individual patients at two local convalescent hospitals one of which had a memory care unit. This was my first-hand encounter to the therapeutic potential of music. I learned a lot about people that summer. I learned about their history and their respective worlds. Some residents were rather quiet, others were very talkative; some preferred listening to their television soap or game show, while others would shut off the television to physically engage with the music as they listened and participated sometimes by singing, humming, clapping, etc. My playing of a piece became *their* music. While most conversations initially centered around music and the guitar, I quickly learned that everyone had their own story and their own collection of songs which connected them to the memories of their youth.

On my very first visit, I vividly remember approaching the door of the single resident's room with my guitar and eagerly introducing myself saying, "Good morning, would you like to hear some music?" She looked up at me, albeit a bit startled, and said curtly "No". I was not prepared for this response. But on my second visit to that facility, the same resident called out to me and asked me into her room. She apologized for not welcoming me, explaining that she had turned me away because she had no money to pay me. I assured her I was only there to play for her enjoyment and not for payment. Over the subsequent weeks and months that passed I looked forward to our visits and conversations. I learned that she was from Texas where she had been an elementary school teacher. One day she asked me to play the song *Yellow Rose of Texas.* I did not know the song. Country western music was not my personal taste of music, but I enthusiastically said I would learn it. In preparing to play her request, I realized a Travis picking pattern (country-folk picking style) would be the best. The *Yellow Rose of Texas* is in a country style and she would be more accustomed to hearing it in that style. When I began playing it for her, she immediately perked up, smiled, and began quietly humming along. Afterwards she asked me, "Do you know who the Yellow Rose of Texas was?" I didn't; I thought the Yellow Rose was *the* flower of Texas. As she explained to me the history of the song as a pre-civil war story about a young courageous woman of color by the name of Emily West, it became clear that I was not simply playing a favorite song of hers: I was generating a memory, a location in time and her own understanding of the world that this particular song preserved for her. My delivery of the piece was a response to her needs and desires. I wasn't there to entertain her. I used my skills on guitar to facilitate an experience that she was directing.

A series of visits with two residents at the same facility also shaped my understanding of music and its therapeutic power. When I first visited the room, one lady sitting in a chair by her bed smiled and welcomed me in to play, while the other lady quietly sat in a chair by the window. There she watched and listened, without saying a word. A month into my weekly visits, that same resident remained silent a mystery to me. She never spoke, even when I spoke to her. When I played the guitar, she would look in my direction, but her eyes appeared to look beyond me. On my fourth visit, I played the flamenco piece Malagueña. Her demeanor suddenly changed. She sat up alertly and began energetically clapping counter rhythms. She softly sang along on during the lyrical bridge. The music had awakened emotional memories in her. When I stopped she spoke to me for the first time: "I remember you! I heard you perform at Carnegie Hall in New York!" While I knew we had never met in New York, from the point on we shared a bond that was introduced through the power of music; I was now a familiar face to her. She would speak to me as if I was an old friend, reminiscing about her life in New York, and, on occasion, asking me to play Malagueña.

These summers were a significant part of my music education as a performer and an educator. Years later, during my tenure in graduate school, I became curious about Music Therapy, which was a new field of music to me. Books, such as Kenneth Brucia's Case Studies in Music Therapy and Improvisational Models of Music Therapy, were part of my extracurricular reading. As I read the individual case studies, I recalled my weekly visits to the convalescent hospitals, and how the power of music inspired, invigorated, and enriched the lives of people I came to know those two summers. A decade later I would have the privilege of working with students at Marylhurst University who aspired to become music therapists. Each student, like those they would serve, had a different story of what brought them to the field of music therapy.

I was initially surprised to learn the guitar was the preferred instrument of most musical therapists and music educators. There are many reasons the guitar is the favored instrument. It is portable, has an extensive timbre palate, and is the most stylistically versatile instrument, bar none. The range of varied rhythmic and timbre variation (strumming, picking, articulation, harmony, pizzicato, harmonics, percussive tones) of the guitar provides the musical therapist and educator a precise and complex musical toolbox. Music - which affects the neural-entrainment processes of brain activity – can influence human behavior, cognition, and emotional processing (Fries, 2005; Melloni et al., 2007; McConnell & Shore, 2011). Drawing from the full scope of the instrument's potential, the musical therapist can select the precise musical tool to heal, educate, uplift, and provide comfort. The goal of this book is to equip you a complete musical toolbox.

Introduction

Music Therapy and Education

The therapeutic use of music in the treatment of physical and mental conditions is called Music Therapy. The ancient origins of using music to treat systemic disorders may be found in the civilizations of the Persians (6000 BCE), the Egyptians (5000 BCE), the Babylonians (1500 BCE), and the Greeks (600 BCE) (Hurley, 2008). Today certified and licensed music therapists employ the latest empirical evidence in crafting music interventions to treat a variety of human needs and conditions. Current research literature has shown the use of music therapy interventions helpful in treatment for physical rehabilitation, facilitating movement, stimulating of memory centers of the brain and improvement of cognitive functioning. Neuroscience research has further shown music activities increase engagement, motivation, and provide a valuable therapeutic emotional outlet (Hurley, 2008).

Of the licensed certified music therapists fifty-five per cent identify the guitar as their clinical instrument, followed by piano (21%), percussion (14%), and other (8%) (Choi, 2008). The continued popularity of guitar in music education has extended to *Music as a Second Language* (MSL) programs (Burnstein and Powell, 2016). The reasons for this preference, beyond a general attraction to the guitar, is portability, the tonal variety of the instrument, and the stylistic versatility the guitar affords the musical therapist. The challenge for non-guitarist music therapy and education students is the acquisition of guitar skills that complement the above mention criteria (Soshensky, 2005). The goal of this book is to provide a thorough and pragmatic methodology that equips the music therapists and educators with the requisite skills to best serve the needs of their clients.

A favorite instrument of sailors and traveling merchants, the guitar's travels literally took it around the world. The guitar was the instrument of the Romani and the Moors. Its popularity among the Portuguese and the Spaniards spread its popularity throughout Europe and the Americas. In the 19th and 20th century the guitar's popularity spread to the East, in countries such as Japan, Korea, Vietnam and the Philippines.

Culturally and stylistically, the guitar is the most stylistically adaptable instrument. The instrument's tonal voice and playing style constitutes a multi-cultural persona: from the percussive flamboyant flamenco style, the mesmerizing Haitian habanera, polyrhythmic Cuban salsa, Argentine tangos, country western ballads, Appalachian folk songs to the Delta blues, jazz, rhythm and blues, rock and roll, and metal rock. The clinical potential of the guitar to cross the cultural and stylistic divide sets it apart. The challenge for the music therapist is in acquiring the necessary foundational and stylistic skills to tap into the therapeutic potential of the multi-cultural persona of the guitar.

The pedagogic approach of this method is uniquely crafted toward achieving this goal. Unlike traditional method books, this book begins with learning foundational guitar skills common to all styles of music. The pace of the material has been thoughtfully structured to help you achieve requisite skill at your pace, while allowing you the creative freedom to musically experiment and apply skills with improvisational impromptus.

Once the foundational skill is achieved students learn soon to read music on the guitar. Chord forms, harmonic progressions, and accompanying formulas are presented in an achievable step-by-step manner. The pace and instructional advice provide a clear path to improve chord changes and master the accompaniment forms.

One of the central goals of this book is to empower you, the music therapist and educator, with skills adaptable to any music (song) you wish to add to your repertoire. This open-ended approach to the repertoire is designed to provide you a multiple of stylistic and clinical options. In your skilled hands music becomes malleable to the clinical needs of the client.

The development of any skill is achieved through practice: observation, self-evaluation, and disciplined effort to improve. Best practice is simple, achievable, easy to repeat, and yields consistent results. Consistency is a form of mastery. The tested and evidence based material of this book will help you develop fluidity of movement, tonal range to affect the emotions of your client and provide the most appropriate accompaniment in your interventions.

This method is the first step. The second companion book, *Musical Styles,* is a treasure chest of right-hand accompaniment templates – from waltz, tango, polka, habanera, and rumba to keyboard ballad, folk-ballad, bluegrass, folk-rock, Gospel, R&B, rock and alternative rock. Each stylistic template can be applied to any song. The easy-to-apply patterns tools are specifically designed to be especially helpful to the knowledgeable music therapist. Employing these patterns to standard chord-progressions can vary the rhythmic accompaniment pattern of any song.

The calculated manipulation of rhythm on guitar can be particularly useful in the use of rhythmic entrainment - auditory rhythmic cues that entrain motor responses. This is particularly important in executing *continuous time reference* (CTR) for period entrainment, which is measured by spatial kinematic and dynamic force of muscle activation that is necessary to producing smooth velocity and acceleration of movement. CTR has been proven useful in treating functional movement disorders (FMDs) (Sievers, Polansky, Casey, & Wheatley, 2013).

These accompaniment patterns can also be used to rhythmically and stylistically enhance songwriting and improvisation interventions/learning activities (instrumental referential, non-referential, song improvisation, vocal non-referential, body improvisation, mixed media, conducted improvisation).

Guitars

The first thing you will notice if you visit a music store to purchase a guitar is how many different types of instruments of guitars there are. While these instruments have much in common, there are many differences in appearance and construction among guitars. While the guitar in the 15th century was as a four-string instrument by the 17th century it had become a five-course guitar had doubled string (much like a 12-string) instrument.

In the late 18th and early 19th century the guitar became a six-string instrument we recognize today. In the late 19th century Spanish luthier Antonio Torres developed a new internal fan-bracing structure which enhanced the tone and increased the dynamic range of the guitar. The Torres guitar was the instrument of choice of the Spanish composer and guitarist Francisco Tárrega.

Over his lifetime Tárrega owned three Torres guitars. His favorite was the 1888 model. Eight years ago, I had the privilege of playing Tárrega's exquisite instrument at the home of master luthier Jeffrey Elliott who had been entrusted to restore the guitar. It was a remarkable instrument with a surprisingly rich and powerful tone. Tárrega was an acclaimed guitar performer and composer. His performances, as was the custom of the time, were chiefly at intimate salon performance settings. In the 20th century maestro Andres Segovia played a Hauser Sr. guitar. Segovia took the guitar from the gentile salon setting to the grand concert halls without electric amplification. Segovia's Hauser guitar was a modified instrument in the Torres tradition.

In the 1830s, cabinet-maker Christian Fredric Martin began making violins under the apprenticeship of Stauffer, and in 1833, he moved to New York where he worked in partnership with other luthiers. His early 1840s guitars are labeled "Martin & Schatz". In the 20th century the Martin company made the first dreadnought style guitar, the first models made for the Oliver Ditson Company. It was until 1931 the instruments had exclusively the Martin name. These instruments were made of mahogany and rosewood. The Martin dreadnought guitars became very popular among folk and bluegrass musicians of the mid-20th century.

The *jumbo body style* was made popular among country-western artists. Elvis played a jumbo body style guitar. It was favored for its bigger resonate tone. Its design however is similar to the dreadnought.

In the quest for a bigger tone *resonator guitars* with one or more resonating metal cones were devised by the Dobyera brothers, more commonly known as the Dobro brothers. Guided by the same goal as the Dobro brothers, the *Selmer-Maccaferri* guitar created a "D"-shaped or longitudinal oval soundhole. This guitar has a bright penetrating tone and is associated with legendary "gypsy" jazz guitarist Django Reinhardt.

Virtuoso guitarist Les Paul - innovative inventor of the electric (amplified) guitars and multitrack recording, and the first looping device - created some of the very first electric pickups for his formerly acoustic Epiphone guitar. With it he single-handedly created a new guitar sound. In 1951 Les Paul further modified his amplified guitar creating the solid-body electric guitar. Today's electric guitars come in myriads of variety (f-hole, V-shape, as well as acoustic-electric folk, flamenco, and classical). Additionally, guitars may be connected to synthesized boxes, pedals, and midi devices giving it access to a multitude of instrument and synthesized sounds.

Picking a Guitar

Students commonly ask what kind of instrument should I purchase? Are all guitars the same? What are the characteristics of a good quality guitar? Is better for me to have a nylon or steel-string guitar? What is the difference between a laminated and solid top instrument? What size a guitar should I play? Should I get a strap? What other devises should I purchase? So many questions?! In the sections below we will examine each of these questions.

Are All Guitars the Same?

The short answer is no. Instruments vary in size and shape of the instrument, the woods used in making the instrument, as well as structural design of the instrument, type (nylon and steel) of strings the instrument was designed for. Each of these differences contribute to the quality of tone, spectrum of tonal timbre available on the instrument, as well as projected dynamic range of the guitar.

A good quality instrument should have a present and balanced tone; i.e., an active mixture of lower and higher frequencies. If an instrument lacks the lower frequencies the tone will be bright and thin. If the lower frequencies dominate the tone will sound muffled and unclear.

Resonance is another desirable quality in a guitar. Like the piano and harp, a struck tone on the guitar is followed by an immediate sharp decay of the intensity of the tone. Master luthiers, makers of guitar, have made great advances in extending the life of a tone. The sustained presence of these new breed of instruments has improved the guitar's ability to improve the singing quality of the instrument.

As with all things, quality comes at a price. A higher quality – tonal balance and dynamic presence – an instrument possesses the more expensive it is. What should you look for in a less expensive quality instrument? The first consideration is the wood used to construct the guitar. It should be a solid-top instrument. The soundboard (the top) is the resonating wood. A quality soundboard is essential to quality instrument. Commonly the top is solid cedar or spruce; the sides and back are typically rosewood or maple. The strings should be comfortably close to the fretboard. If the strings are too high from the fingerboard it is harder to avoid unpleasant buzzes. Quality instruments are not more difficult to play, they are more responsive to the player. So, what is the low-end price of an excellent starting instrument? The price of a reasonably priced solid-top guitar ranges from $300 - $600.

Does Size Matter?

Yes, while the standard scale length of guitars varies, size does matter. Size of the guitar determines the tone, dynamics, and comfort (ease) in playing the instrument. The choice, therefore, of size and type (nylon or steel string, acoustic or electric) is individual. Choosing an instrument is determined by the player's physical characteristics and personal taste.

Playability is an important consideration in picking an instrument. The string length, width of the neck, and the *action* (i.e., string's distance from the fretboard) contribute to the ease in learning to play guitar. The longer the string the greater the distance between frets. The wider the neck the further the fingers have to stretch across the strings to finger chords. The higher the strings are from the fingerboard the greater the strength is required to push the string down.

A nylon ("classical") guitar has a scale length of 650 millimeters; the scale length of a steel string guitar is typically 610 millimeters (approximately 22 inches). Why the difference in string length? String length commonly affects the tone quality and dynamic response of an instrument. The string tension on smaller scale length instruments typically are less taut to finger; they have a softer and deeper sounding tone. Longer scale length instruments typically have greater string tension, resulting in a brighter piercing tone quality.

Steel-string guitars are brighter in their tone quality. The physical property of nylon strings is substantially different than steel strings. Steel is less flexible than nylon. Nylon strings feel softer to the touch than steel. The diameter of a nylon string is larger than a steel string. Because of this, nylon string instruments require a longer string length to increase the string tension sufficiently so it does not rattle against the fingerboard. Steel strings do not require as much tension to achieve comparable results. Nylon-string guitars offer more variety of tonal color than steel-string guitars. Steel-string guitars have a brighter and penetrating tone quality.

The action of a nylon string instrument is commonly higher (greater) than a steel string. The higher action increases the string tension making the effort (strength) required to finger notes on a nylon strings comparable to that of steel-string guitar with lower string action. While the effort to get a clear tone of the two instruments is comparable, the softer texture of the larger nylon strings is generally experienced as gentler on the fingertips than steel strings.

Parlor guitars are smaller steel string instruments. They are excellent instruments for those with smaller hands and prefer a warmer midrange tone quality. They also make good instruments for children.

Steel string or Nylon?

We return to the third question: Is better for me to have a nylon or steel-string guitar? There is no easy answer. The choice of instruments is matter of individual taste. The best recommendation, therefore, is to take some time to make the decision yourself. Considerations of ease to play may lead you to prefer nylon over steel, or the smaller thinner neck of a parlor guitar over a wider nylon-string instrument.

The tonal nuances among different guitar types and specific makers of guitars will become more apparent in time. Tonal preferences may be influenced by the style of music. Preferences may be influenced by the tonal preferences of your client. A Japanese music therapist assigned to brain trauma patients in a hospital reported some clients preferred the tone of a natural piano to an electric keyboard. Some clients may prefer fuller warmer tone to a brighter tone. See https://youtu.be/W_0Mu-JGM40 .

Parts of the Guitar

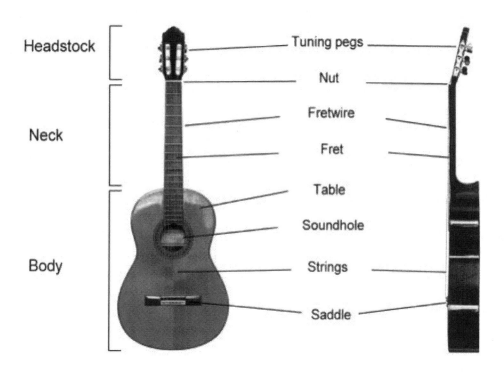

Tuning Your Guitar

Sound (bombarding air molecules) travels in the form of a longitudinal waves. The wave length corresponds to individual periods of oscillation of air pressure. The frequency of these oscillations (sound waves) we experience as pitch. Each musical tone corresponds to a frequency of pitch which is measures in hertz, in honor of the Heinrich Hertz who discovered electromagnetic waves.

Until the early 19th century there was no universal standard of pitch. Tuning a consort of instruments consequently varied from region to region. In 1830s Johann Heinrich Scheibler, a silk manufacturer and self-taught musicologist, created a *tonometer*; a series of 56 tuning forks that measured pith. Scheibler recommended 440 vibrations per second (Hz) as the standard of pitch for the tone **A**. It was not until the 1930s that A 440Hz became the "universal standard of pitch". See https://youtu.be/_wIho1S3pSU .

Tuning Guitar to the Piano

If you have a piano you may tune the six open strings of a guitar from the lowest to the highest pitch are E, A, D, G, B, and E to the piano. The first two open bass strings are below middle C (see below) on the piano. The fourth, third, second, and first open strings are above middle C (see below). The distance (interval) between the open strings, with the exception of the third and second string, is a perfect fourth (four notes): E (f, g) A, A (b, c) D, D (e, f) G, and B (c, d) E. The distance between third and second string is a third: G (a) B.

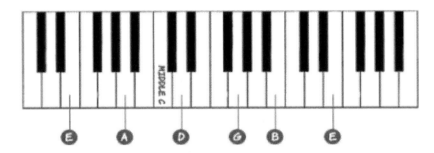

If you have a piano that is in tune, you may tune the guitar by matching the pitches of the piano (as shown above) to the open strings of the guitar. Using the right pedal of the piano will cause the tone to continue to sustain after you strike it freeing your hand to play, compare and match the pitch of the guitar to the piano. It may be helpful to strike the string repeatedly as you compare and determine by ear whether the two tones are in tune or whether the guitar is higher or lower. If the string is lower turn the sixth string key toward you the raise the pitch, away from you to lower the pitch. Continue to strike the string and compare the tones to determine when they are in tune.

Relative Tuning

If you do not have a piano, you may tune the guitar relative to itself. Assuming the sixth string is in tune, proceed to the fifth fret of the sixth string. Pluck and compare the sixth string fifth fret to the open fifth string; both notes should be the same pitch (A). If the open fifth string is lower turn the sixth string key toward you the raise the pitch, away from you to lower the pitch. The tuning of each of the next strings is accomplished in the same fashion. The open fourth string should match fifth string fifth fret. The open third should match the fourth string fifth fret, and the first string open the second string fifth fret. The tuning of the second string is the exception. The open second string should match the third string fourth fret. This again is because the interval (distance) between the open third and second (G to B) is three notes away instead of four.

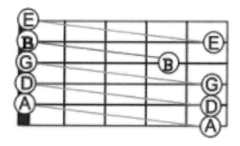

This method of tuning is not as easy to compare and adjust as using the piano or an electronic tuner. When you move your hand to adjust the tuning key the fingered tone ceases to sound. You have to remember desired tone of the fingered tone to determine and adjust the tone of the ringing open string accordingly. Another subtle complication is the fingered tone has a fuller deeper tone quality than the open string. This can make it harder to match the tones comparatively. You may judge the fingered tone to be lower in pitch than it is.

Electronic Tuners

The simplest and most accurate tuning tool is the electronic tuner. There are two varieties those that clip on to the head of the guitar and those that are placed in front of the guitar. There are also convenient tuning apps for your phone that very effective. Electronic tuning devices calculate the tone's wavelength (Hrz). Be sure the device is set to determine pitch with A equal to 440 Hrz. (Some areas of the world have a higher standard of pitch where A equals 444 or 446). Then comparing to this note to desired pitch, a needle on the tuner's meter shows how low or high the note is compared to the desired tone; the 0 spot in the center of the screen. If the tone is flat (low), the needle on the meter will be in the left hemisphere; if it is sharp (higher) it will be in the right hemisphere. When the tone is "in tune" it will be centered on the 0 spot. Most attached tuners use a red colored light on the right or left hemisphere to indicate if the tone is flat or sharp. A green light is used to indicate the note is in tune.

Recommendation for Ear Training

As stated above the easiest and fastest method to tune your instrument is an electronic tuner. While this method is the easiest, it does have its drawbacks. In the event the device does not operate due to low battery or malfunction you will need to rely on your own skill to tune your instrument. This is a good reason to develop the ability to differentiate pitch and tune the guitar without a tuning device. Ear training, pitch identification, is an important skill for all musicians.

Guitar Maintenance

Cleanliness

Guitar maintenance monitors the guitar condition and protects the instrument from harm. Much of the following reminders may seem like common sense. Nevertheless, better a healthy reminder than presumed knowledge. The safest place for the guitar when it is not being played is in the case. When removing the guitar from the case hold the top of the case with one hand as you carefully lift the guitar from the case. Guitar stands may be convenient when you need to momentarily need put the guitar down. It is best even in these cases you are close by to protect the guitar from harm. If the guitar falls and strikes the ground it can be badly damaged costing hundreds of dollars to repair.

When you play guitar, dirt and grease from your hands can collect as grime on the guitar surface. As easy remedy is to wipe the guitar down with a cleaning cloth after playing your instrument. Guitar cleaning clothes can be purchased at most music stores. Wipe the strings and the frets. Such daily cleaning protects the guitar from environmental and usage effects.

Heat and Humidity

When traveling or storing the guitar try to keep changes in temperature moderate. Sudden changes in temperature and humidity can damage the wood, sometimes causing cracks or loosening of internal braces. Monitor the conditions of the guitar. Prevent sudden changes in heat and humidity. Don't leave the guitar in the trunk of a car on a hot or cold day. Try to keep the temperature controlled when moving from the car to a house or vice versa.

When to Change Strings

When the strings become worn the intonation and dynamic responsiveness is compromised. The length of time between string changes demands largely on how often and long you play the instrument. If you practice 45 - 60 minutes a day, you should change the strings at least twice a year. Double that amount of practice, and you should expect to change the strings every three months. Professional musicians change the strings more frequently, as often as twice a month.

Accessing the Videos

There are a number of videos cited in the text. These give the student the opportunity to see and hear important parts of each lesson. In the ebook version of this book the reader merely clicks on the link and the video appears on your computer or tablet—naturally you must be connected to the Internet. For those of you reading the print version of the book, merely write the link address into your address bar.

How is this method book different?

Unlike traditional guitar instructional books, this book is specifically written for music therapy and education students. The pedagogic method employed focuses on mastering three central goals: **skills, literacy, and versatility.**

Skills

Skill development (*know how*) is teaching your body how to play the guitar (sound technique or mechanics). In the first step, the student learns how to position their hand and independently control the movement of the fingers - tools which are indispensable to advancement and proficiency on any instrument. The early exercises and musical studies are simple, easy to memorize, and yet challenging to execute correctly. Early melodic pieces allow students the option of engaging in some "improvising"; namely, changing the order and rhythm of the notes. This improvisatory addendum to the studies (Impromptus) makes skill development an engaging and enjoyable creative activity. Much of the early exercises have harmonic accompaniments available for the student to practice, again, making the exercises a more musically satisfying experience.

Literacy

Many students of the guitar struggle with note reading. In the thirty years of teaching Zisa has met many advanced players of guitar who struggle with music literacy and have not learned to read music. The pedagogic approaches to music literacy (reading of music notation) in this book is innovative and creative. Ninety percent of students who struggle with note reading become excellent sight readers after following the course material in this book. The hypothesis is learning to read music is like learning a written language. When learning a language, you first learn to say the word, then - you learn to read it. This is not the methodology of 99% of instructional books for guitar.

The method approach of this book treats music as a language. First the student learns the placement and names of the fingered notes. Then they learn how the note is notated. This method approach has three steps: Play and say, read and say, read and play. Step one, *play and say,* teaches the location and names of the fingered note. Step two, *read and say*, focuses solely on reading and identifying the letter names of the notes. The speed and ease of note identification leads naturally into the third and final step. Step three, *Read and play,* students read-see-and play the written music. Because the hand and fingers are properly positioned over the notes, the execution of this last step is comparatively easy.

Versatility

Given the curriculum demands on first and second year students, the most difficult area of their musical development is versatility. Because music therapists use the guitar primarily as an accompanying instrument, this method advances the knowledge and skills that would be most advantageous in the areas of harmony, rhythm, dynamics, and style. Versatility in harmony affects mood. In rhythm, versatility impacts energy and engagement. The use of varied dynamics affects engagement and mood. Stylistic differences affect the character of the music. This method helps students attain the necessary physical skills, literacy, and versatility on the guitar.

Lesson 1: Acquiring the Know-How

Before you learned the rules of baseball or played your first game, someone first taught you how throw the ball. I can still remember the day my father took me out to the back yard and taught me how to throw. My first efforts were not pretty or successful. I was right handed. He told I needed to put my left foot in the front of the right foot. It simply did not feel natural to do it that way. Initially I resisted. After numerous efforts and meager results, he told me to practice shifting my weight from my back (right) foot forward toward my left foot. Then he told me to mirror this movement with my arm movement and follow through past my ear and beyond my stationary left foot. This was not easy. I still found myself back on the wrong foot.

This may sound familiar to you if can remember **how** you came to learn **how** to throw a ball. Mastering this complex coordinated movement of your body was critical to your success. Acquiring the skill was no easy matter. It was not achieved in an hour or a single day. At this time of your life, you may not remember the particulars of your process of learning: the many failed efforts, points of partial success, or the monumental moment when you achieved success. This skill empowered you with the **know-how** to throw the ball for speed and distance.

Acquiring guitar skills follows similar principles. Skill development is acquiring **know-how**. As with learning to throw a ball playing the guitar is not a natural skill, it is a learned skill. When you master a skill, your **know-how** becomes second nature to you; that is, it is so natural you don't have to think about it. An accomplished typist does not have to look at their hands. Their hands seem to dance effortlessly across the keyboard. Much the same way, musicians' relation to their instrument appears to be a natural appendage to their body.

This lesson is the first step in acquiring this **know how** on the guitar. **Know how** is turning knowledge into skill. The process begins with you learning **what** you need to do, then teaching yourself step-by-step **how** to do it. The role of a teacher and a good method book should also provide helpful feedback and recommendations in **how** to develop this skill. Sometimes it is necessary to master a single skill before combining it with other components in the developmental process. For example, before you can position your hand correctly you need to learn how to hold your instrument. Each acquired skill increases your **know-how** and takes you one step closer to your goal.

Before reading on and beginning this exciting adventure, take time to reflect what your goals are. If you aspire to use music in a therapeutic setting, reflect on what skills you will need. If you wish to use the guitar as an educator, consider how you envision using the guitar in an educational setting. How do you hope to impact your students' knowledge and experience of music? How the guitar will compliment your efforts? For over forty years I have helped aspiring guitarists on this journey. This method provides offers a friendly path to success.

Holding the guitar

When playing the guitar, it is important for your posture to be balanced and relaxed. Your shoulders should be aligned and straight. Leaning forward slightly, your back should be lifted and straight. Hold the guitar so head of the head of the instrument is shoulder or eye-level. This is best achieved placing an adjustable footstool under the left foot or using guitar support, which attaches to the guitar to raise the guitar. Bend the arm at the elbow keeping the forearm through the wrist straight, and the aligning the fingers even with the frets.

Having positioned the guitar in your lap, position the left-hand fingers on string four with the first finger behind the seventh fret (seventh position). String four is the fourth string from the bottom, third from the top. Each finger (1, 2, 3, 4) should be positioned on frets 7, 8, 9, and 10 respectively, with the thumb flat behind the second finger (fret 8).

The fingers should be curved with the tip-joint of each finger perpendicular to the fingerboard. Push the string down the fingertip slightly above the fret. Note: the position is marked by placement of the first finger on the fingerboard. When the first finger is behind fret one you are in position one. In position seven, the first finger is behind the seventh fret.

Exercises

1: Lift/Place

2: walk down

3: patterns

Left hand exercises

The following exercises are intended fo[illegible] allow you the opportunity to devote 100% of your attention [illegible]on and gaining independent control of the movement of the fi[illegible]ow are arranged in order of difficulty. After devoting 10 minutes [illegible]e encouraged to explore playing the three improvisation (improve) studies. See https://youtu.be/ABph7FWpQ1s .

Exercise 1

Exercise 1 consist of three four-finger patterns. The goal is to establish independence of movement and to maintain the position of the fingers above the fourth string on the designated frets. Begin by setting the fingers on the fourth string in seventh position. Be sure the fingers (1, 2, 3, 4) are on the seventh, eighth, ninth, and ten frets respectively. The thumb should be positioned behind the eighth fret. When the position of the fingers is established, lift them above the fourth string. Maintain each finger's position over designated frets as you execute the pattern. If a finger feels weak, moves out of position, or presses against another finger, be sure to repeatedly correct the error until maintaining the position becomes second nature.

Pattern 1: Place 1 down, add 2, lift 1, add 3, lift 2, add 4, lift 3.

Pattern 2: Place 1 down, add 3, lift 1, add 2, lift 3, add 4, lift 2.

Pattern 3: Place 1 down, add 4, lift 1, add 2, lift 4, add 3, lift 2.

Exercise 2

Exercise 2 is a kind of spider walk across the fretboard beginning on the fourth string. The goal is to maintain finger position as you transition from string to string, beginning on string four and ending on string one. The fingers should remain in the same fret positions throughout. Begin by setting the fingers on the fourth string in seventh position, as you did in Exercise 1. Leaving the fingers on the fourth string, move the first finger to string 3. Follow this by slowly moving each individual finger (2, 3, 4) to string 3. The hand position should move away the distance one string from the side of the neck. While doing this critically observe the hand position or stability of the finger movement to see if it changes or is compromised. If a finger feels weak, moves out of position, or presses against another finger, be sure to repeatedly correct the error until transitioning to and from adjacent strings is second nature. Keep the elbow down arm and the wrist straight. Each finger should move independently.

Exercise 3

Exercise 3 is a two-finger pattern across the fretboard from the fourth string to the first string and back. The goal is to smoothly transition from string to string like a scale and maintain the positioning of the two inactive digits. Scale patterns on the guitar consist of two-finger and three-finger combinations. The simplicity of the exercise allows you the player opportunity to focus your entire attention on how each finger is impacted while executing the two-finger pattern. In this way, you can isolate and master each two-finger combination. If a finger is weak it may lean against another digit. Additionally, the inactive fingers may move away from the desired position or simply lift further from the fingerboard. Correcting these natural undesired tendencies requires slowing the pace to allow yourself enough time to consciously override the natural impulses. Repeated effort to maintain individual control of the finger position will result in consistent results (mastery).

      Pattern 1: 1-2, 1-2, 1-2, 1-2
      Pattern 2: 1-3, 1-3, 1-3, 1-3
      Pattern 3: 1-4, 1-4, 1-4, 1-4
      Pattern 4: 2-3, 2-3, 2-3, 2-3
      Pattern 5: 2-4, 2-4, 2-4, 2-4
      Pattern 6: 3-4. 3-4, 3-4, 3-4

Improvisation Pieces

The Impromptu Studies below are easy to memorize melodic patterns on two and three strings. The tones used are part of a pentatonic (five-tone) scale pattern. The melodic pattern (1-4, 2-4 respectively) of Impromptu 1 moves from string one and two over the course of two measures. Because the pattern is simple to memorize you can watch your left-hand position and the position of the fingers.

The notes may be played gently with the thumb. Each tone may be held for two beats. When playing the pattern becomes easier to control and play, you may shorten the time value of the tones. The technical challenge in the Impromptu pieces lies in mastering fingering changes. The musical challenge is to change the pattern and create your own melodies. Instructional instruction and chordal accompaniment to Impromptu 1 may be found at https://youtu.be/7kTlbOtrPX4 .

Impromptu 1

	Measure 1	Measure 2	Measure 3	Measure 4
String 1	1 - 4	1 - 4		
String 2			2 - 4	2 - 4

Impromptu 2 changes strings and fingering pattern every measure as opposed to every other measure. This makes Impromptu 2 more challenging. Again, once the left-hand finger pattern is mastered, then students should try to creatively vary the pattern and create a melody of their own. Instructional chordal accompaniment to Impromptu 2 may be found at https://youtu.be/o9GT6u8WvBY .

Impromptu 2

	Measure 1	Measure 2	Measure 3	Measure 4
String 1	1 - 4		1 - 4	
String 2		2 - 4		2 - 4

Impromptu 3 adds another string and two-finger pattern (1-3 on string three). This completes the five-tone pentatonic scale pattern. These new two-tones tones add to the difficulty and allow for more creative possibilities.

Impromptu 3

	Measure 1	Measure 2	Measure 3	Measure 4
String 1	1 - 4			
String 2		2 - 4		2 - 4
String 3			1 - 3	

Lesson 1 Practice Calendar

Two Goals:

(1) Establish left-hand position; independence of movement; improve control.

(2) Establish right-hand position, achieve proper distance from the string; develop consistency in carrying out the five parts of the stroke.

	Sunday	Monday	Tuesday	Wednesday	Thursday	Friday	Saturday
Scales							
Chords							
Arpeggio							
Strum							
New Songs							
Old Songs							

Practice - minimum of 20 minutes per day

Left hand - 10 minute twice per day

(1) Left hand Exercise 1, 2, 3 (5 minutes per day)

(2) Impromptus 1, 2, & 3 (5 minutes per day)

Lesson 2: Rhythm: the Dance of Time

The nature of rhythm is movement in time. This movement is defined by an evenly occurring pulse (beat). A full beat is divided into two parts: the downbeat and the upbeat. The most fundamental physical component of rhythm of a beat is its dancelike movement which occurs between the points in time when the foot touches the ground (the down beat) and when the foot is at its apex in midair (the upbeat). A full beat extends from the downbeat to downbeat, or upbeat to upbeat.

Downbeat   Upbeat   **Down**beat   Upbeat

Walk in step to the beat of music. Observe the feeling of when your foot touches the ground as compared to when it is apex in midair. Bend your knees and feel the weight of the beat. Move your arms down and up to the beat. Feel the weight of a down beat. When you lift your arms feel the lightness of the upbeat. A full beat may be described as occurring between the points in time from one downbeat to another, or from one upbeat to another.

Meter

Another characteristic of rhythm is described as **meter**: *the pattern of stressed and unstressed beats.* The experience of a stressed downbeat followed by an unstressed downbeat is perceived as a two-beat pattern; a two-beat pattern is called a simple duple meter. Marches are typically in simple duple meter.

Down	Up	Down	Up
1		2	
Right foot		Left foot	

Rhythm Notation

Music notation is a set of music symbols representing rhythm and pitch. One symbol used to represent a beat is called a quarter note. A full beat may be divided into two parts: extending from down beat to down beat, or upbeat to upbeat.

The two quarter notes below represent two tones, each is sustained for a full beat (downbeat to downbeat). In a two-beat (duple) pattern the sound on beat one would be louder (greater intensity) than beat two.

Down	Up	Down	Up
1		2	
♩		♩	

If a tone sounds from the downbeat to the next upbeat, or from an upbeat to the next downbeat, its sustained time value would be half a beat. A symbol used to notate a half a beat is an eighth note. Four eighth notes are equal to the time value of two quarter notes.

Down	Up	Down	Up
1		2	
♪	♪	♪	♪

Measures and Bar Lines

A measure in time is defined by the meter beat pattern. A simple duple meter has two beats in each measure. A measure is a unit of time. A vertical bar line is the symbol used to indicate the end of measure and the beginning of the next measure. Examine the four-bar rhythm in simple duple meter below. Note the placement of the vertical bar line separates each two-beat pattern. In the final measure a double-bar line is used to indicate the last measure.

Compose a Rhythm Song!

Compose a four-bar rhythm piece. Begin (step 1) by using the words *down* and *up* to create a catchy rhythm of quarter notes and eighth notes. When you find a rhythmic word pattern you like, write it down just as you spoke it out aloud. Draw bar lines to separate each group of two-beat rhythm pattern.

Step two write below the words the rhythmic equivalent. Down, followed by a silent up, becomes a quarter note. Down and up become two eighth notes (see following example).

Example:

step 1	Down (up) Down (up)	Down up Down (up)	Down up Down up	Down (up) Down (up)
step 2	♩ ♩	♪ ♪ ♩	♪ ♪ ♪ ♪	♩ ♩

Strumming: The Dance of the Right Hand

The nature of strumming is movement in time. The strum movement is associated to the dancelike movement of the foot touching the ground (the down beat) and upward movement of the foot when its apex in midair (the upbeat). When strumming on the down beats (quarter notes) move your foot and body to pulse of your rhythm strumming dance. A full beat extends from the downbeat to downbeat, or upbeat to upbeat.

Two Chords

Em is an E-minor chord. To finger an E-minor chord place the first finger on the fifth string behind the second fret (this note is a B), and your second finger on string 4 behind fret 2 ("E"). Strum all six strings with the index finger in a downward motion from lowest sounding string (string 6) to the highest (string 1). Strum the chord slowly and gently to confirm all the chord tones sound clearly.

Cmaj7 is a C major seventh chord. Place the third finger on string 5 behind the third fret ("C"), and your second finger on string four behind fret 2 ("E"). Strum all five strings with the index finger in a downward motion from second lowest sounding string (string 5) to the highest (string 1). Strum the chords slow and gently to confirm all the chord tones sound clearly. See https://youtu.be/pMjh2trLmF0 .

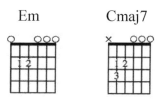

Exercise 1

Using the right index finger to strum down on the down beat, sounding for one full beat and notated as a quarter note as shown in Exercise 1. Rock the body and move the foot in synchronized movement with the index strumming the Em or Cmaj7.

Down	Up	Down	Up
1		2	
♩		♩	

Exercise 2

Fingering Em or Cmaj7 gently strum up with the index finger on the top treble strings (the three upper strings). Strumming up on the upbeat (eighth notes) as shown in Exercise 2. Rock the body and move the foot in synchronized movement with the beat. Feel the upward movement of the index finger strumming on the top three treble strings as the upbeat.

Down	Up	Down	Up
1		2	
rest	♪	rest	♪

Exercise 3

Combine the two movements in strumming E minor or a Cmaj7 chord to continuous eighth notes. This will result in a full downward strum (all chord tones) on the down beat and lighter up strum on the treble (top three) strings on the up-beat. Rock the body and foot movement in a synchronized movement with the hand, feeling and strumming the E minor chord.

Down	Up	Down	Up
1		2	
♪	♪	♪	♪

Exercise 4

After you have a command of the right-hand movement in executing a full downward strum and the lighter up strum, practice changing chord fingering for Em and Cmaj7. Moving from Em to Cmaj7 add the third finger without moving the first finger. Simply lift the third finger when moving back to Em. Remember all six strings sound on the full downward strum when fingering the Em chord and only five strings (string five to one) sound on the downbeats for Cmaj7. Practice synchronizing the movement of chord changes with the timing of the strum.

Em		C maj7	
Down up Down up	Down up Down up	Down up Down up	Down up Down up
♩ ♪ ♪	♩ ♪ ♪	♩ ♪ ♪	♩ ♪ ♪

Em		C maj7	
Down up Down up	Down up Down up	Down up Down up	Down up Down up
♪ ♪ ♩	♪ ♪ ♩	♪ ♪ ♩	♪ ♪ ♩

Arpeggio

The word arpeggio comes from the Italian verb *arpeggiare*, to pluck the strings like a harp. On guitar this is commonly accomplished by holding a chord form with the left hand while the right hand plucks a sequence of strings (overlapping chord tones). While the chord tones are struck individually the resulting combined tones continues to resonate, resulting in a harmonious blend of tones. Typically right hand fingers strike the string in a free-stroke (tirando) manner so not to stop the adjacent strings from ringing. Follow four minutes of direction on https://youtu.be/RjLl1q3QFx4 .

Establish the Position

(1) Establish the right-hand position with fingers relaxed above the strings.
   Rest the thumb (p) gently on the third string.
   The top-knuckle of the index finger should be forward over string two, and top-knuckle of the middle finger should be over string one.
(2) Extend finger and touch string with left side of fingertip.
(3) With a combination of nail and flesh push down and across the string.
   The momentum of follow-through should move the fingertip past the adjacent string.
(4) When the forward motion stops, allow the finger to return to "ready" position.
(5) Skill is achieved through observation, self-evaluation, and a determined effort to

improve.

(6) Keep practice routine simple to achieve success. Build on success until it is easy to repeat and yields you consistent results. Consistency is a form of mastery!

Pattern 1 and 2

Practice the right hand alone patterns below on open strings initially. The thumb (p) should be lightly positioned on the third string. There are two right-hand finger patterns below:

(1) i - m - i - m pattern on strings two and one respectively, and

(2) m-i-m-i pattern on strings one and two respectively.

Pattern 1

String 1		m		m
String 2	i		i	

Pattern 2

String 1	m		m	
String 2		i		i

Jacob's Ladder

This simple piece is in first position. The string numbers refer to frets: "0" is open string; "2" is fret 2. Fingered notes may be played with one or two fingers.

		i	m	i	m	i	m	i	m	i	m	i	m	i	m	i
String 1		0		2		3	2		0		3		2			
String 2	0		0		0			0		0		0		0	0	0

	m	i	m	i	m	i	m	i	m	i	m	i	m	i
String 1	0		2		3		2		0	3	2	0		
String 2		0		0		0		0					0	0	0

Be creative with Jacob's Ladder, improvise, and create new melodies.

Lesson 2 Practice Calendar

Two Goals:

(3) Learn and apply concepts of meter & rhythm as related to quarter note and eighth note strumming.

(2) Master chords E minor (Em) and C-major seventh (C maj7). Quick and accurate chord changes.

	Sunday	Monday	Tuesday	Wednesday	Thursday	Friday	Saturday
Scales							
Chords							
Arpeggio							
Strum							
New Songs							
Old Songs							

Practice - minimum of 30 minutes per day

Scales: 5 minutes per day
Left exercise two and three
Play each tone twice alternating right-hand fingering; e.g., i - m - i m.

Right hand two note arpeggio patterns: 5 minutes per day
(1) "i - m - i - m" and "m - i - m -i"
(2) Jacob's Ladder – (One-finger Etude) to "i - **m** - i – m – I" pattern

Chord changes - 5 minutes per day
    (1) Learn two chords: E minor and C major seventh.
    (2) Synchronized movement - fingers move and arrive at the same time.
    (3) Legato - maintain an even rhythm when changing chords between measures
    (4) Coordinate chord changes with the strum or picking

Strum Patterns - 5 minutes
    (1) Two patterns a day
    (2) Accurate rhythm of the strum with index finger
    (3) Strike correct number of strings
    (4) Aim for a full down strum, and light up strung

Song repertoire - 10 minutes
    (1) 5 minutes on the strum patterns for exercise four and piece Jacob's Ladder.
    (2) 5 minutes on learned repertoire (Impromptu 1, 2, 3).

Lesson 3: Music Notation

Music notation is a specialized form of music writing to communicate how pitch (sound frequency), tone (quality of sound), tempo (rate of the beat), dynamics (intensity of pitch), and articulation (the manner a series of tones are produced in relationship to each other). Traditional western notation employs a clef in conjunction with a five-line (four space) grid to assign pitch. The treble clef is used for guitar. Pitch is indicated by the head (the oval shaped portion of the written note) on, above, or below the staff. Each pitch is given a letter name.

There are seven names in the musical alphabet: A, B, C, D, E, F, and G. Vertical (bar) lines separate and organize tones into measures. A double bar indicates the completion of a section of music; whereas, the final double bar appears at the conclusion of the piece of music.

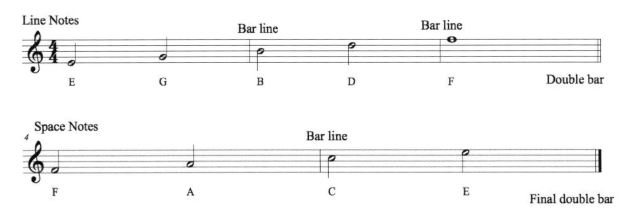

Rhythm and Note Types

The appearance of a note indicates duration. Notes are made up of two parts: the head (circle shape portion) of the note and the stem. The head of **quarter note** is black with a stem (an upward or downward line). The head of an **eighth note** is also black; a flag at the end of the stem differentiates an eighth note from a quarter note. Additionally, two eighth notes commonly have a beam connecting the stem ends. The head of a **half note** is not colored and has a stem. While the head of a **whole note** is not colored; it has no stem. The proportional value of a note types is how duration is determined. For example, if a quarter note equals one beat, then the proportional value of a half note is two beats, a whole note equals four beats, and the smaller eighth note equals half a beat.

Time Signatures

The fraction-like symbol appearing at the beginning of a composition is called the time signature. The time signature provides the performer two important pieces of information: The number of beats per bar (measure), and the type of note designated to receive one beat. In **2/4 time**, for example, the upper number indicates there are **two beats per bar (measure)**; the lower number indicates a quarter note is equal to one beat. There are four beats per bar in 4/4 time; a quarter note equals one beat.

Rests

Rests are used to indicate periods of silence.

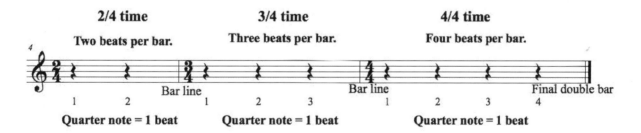

Meter and Time Signatures

The meter is a descriptive of the rhythmic pulse of the music. A pattern of two occurs when the first pulse is emphasized pulse and second pulse is unstressed. Such a pattern is described as a **duple meter. 2/4 time** is an example of duple meter.

A three-beat pattern, a stressed beat followed by two unstressed beats, is **triple meter. 3/4 time** is an example of triple meter. A four-beat pattern is **quadruple meter. 4/4 time** is an example of quadruple meter.

Rhythm: The Dance of Time

Common Time: Quadruple Meter

Simple quadruple duple meter places dynamic emphasis on the first and third downbeat. The second and fourth downbeats are unstressed. The difference between quadruple and duple meters is the third beat in quadruple meter is less stressed than beat one. Distinguishing the difference between duple and quadruple meter may be likened to comparing the word **ho**ney (duple) to **pea**nut **but**ter (quadruple). Simple quadruple meter is also referred to as Common Time because it is "commonly" used in western music.

The time signature for common time (simple quadruple meter) is 4/4 time. The top number of the time signature indicates there are four beats per bar; the bottom number identifies a quarter note as equal to one beat. When strumming on the downbeat in 4/4 time the first and third beat in quadruple meter receive the strongest accent, the second and fourth beat are not accented.

Simple Quadruple Time and Strumming

The time value of half notes and whole notes are proportionally longer than quarter notes. A half note is twice the time value than a quarter note; a whole note is four times as long. If a quarter note equals one beat, then a half note equals two beats and a whole note four beats long.

Etude 1

The rhythm of the strum below combines a quarter notes, half notes, and whole notes. While all the strums below fall on the down beat, it is important to continue to rock your body and tap your foot to mark and feel each down and upbeat. **The letter "D" below the written rhythms represents a down strum, and "U" an up strum.**

Etude 1 ~ Rhythmic Strumming

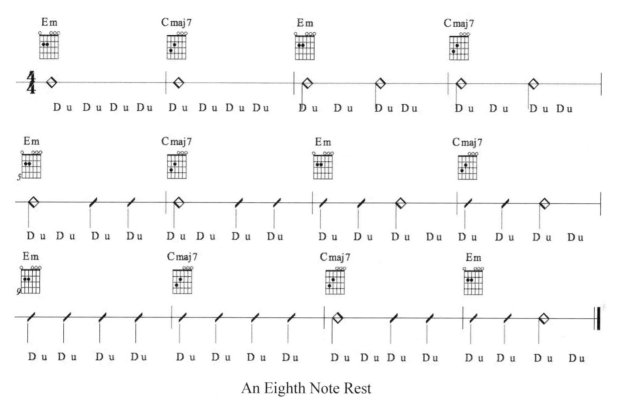

An Eighth Note Rest

The measure below has an eighth note rest (half a beat of silence) on the down beats. The strums consequently are played on the upbeat.

Upbeat Strum

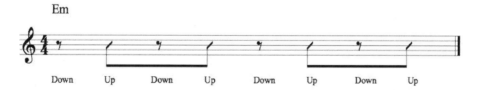

Etude 2

Each line below is a four-measure strum pattern. Each line pattern should be practiced to gain mastery (control of the chord changes and precise rhythmic execution of the strum). Rock the body and move the foot in synchronized movement with the hand to coordinate the rhythm with the strumming. Strive not to interrupt the rhythm of this movement when changing chords. Strumming quarter and eighth notes follow directions: https://youtu.be/gSgqg_wCyBg .

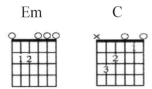

Etude 2 ~ Rhythmic Strumming

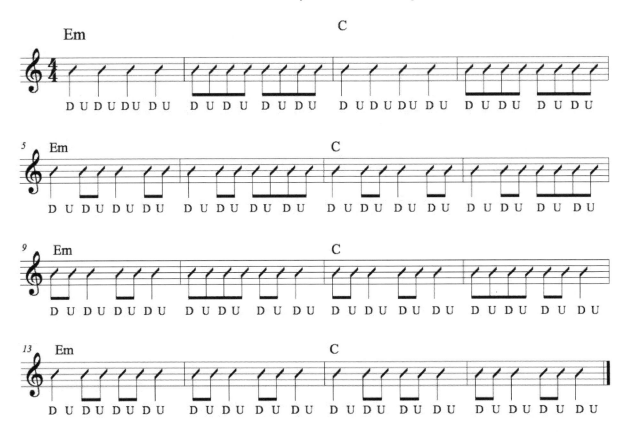

The following song uses two chords: Em and C. The C chord is different from the C major-seventh in that the first finger is positioned on string two, fret one. On the first line, each chord is struck once and held for eight beats. The song uses one four-beat measure strum pattern on the second, third, and fourth system. Again, rock the body and move the foot in synchronized movement with the hand to coordinate the rhythm with the strumming. Again, the letter "D" below the rhythm notation represents a down strum, and "U" an up strum. Strive not to interrupt the rhythm of this movement when changing chords. Coincidentally, the chords of this song are same as the Beatle Song "Eleanor Rigby". **The letter "D" represents a down strum, and "U" an up strum.**

Quiet Desperation

Peter Joseph Zisa

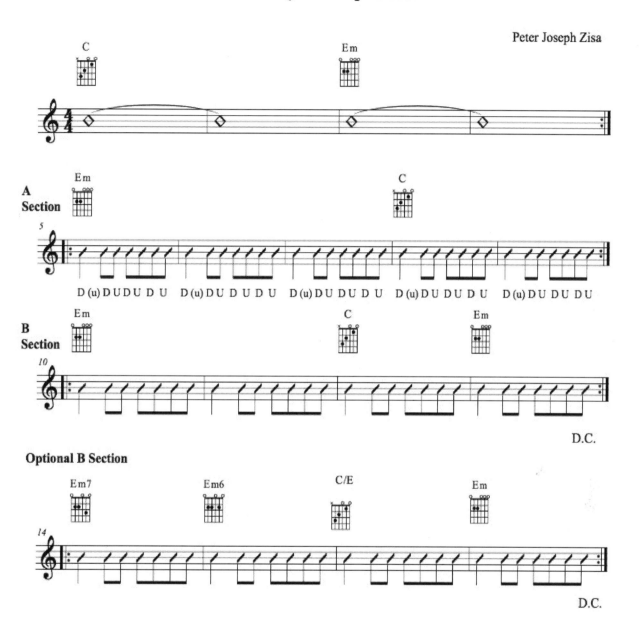

Arpeggio

As noted earlier, the word arpeggio comes from the Italian verb *arpeggiare*, to pluck the strings like a harp. This is commonly accomplished on guitar by holding a chord form with the left hand while the right hand plucks a sequence of strings. The tones are struck individually, each resulting tone continues to resonate resulting in a harmonious blend of tones. Typically, the right-hand fingers strike the string in a free-stroke (tirando) manner so not to stop the adjacent strings from ringing.

Establish the Foundation

(1) Establish right hand position with fingers relaxed above the strings.
　Rest the thumb (p) gently on the third string.
　The top-knuckle of the index finger should be forward over string two, and top-knuckle of the middle finger should be over string one.
(2) Extend finger and touch string with left side of fingertip.
(3) With a combination of nail and flesh push down and across the string.
The momentum of follow-through should move the fingertip past the adjacent string.
(4) When the forward motion stops, allow the finger to return to "ready" position.
(5) Skill is achieved through observation, self-evaluation, and a determined effort to improve.
(6) Keep practice routine simple to achieve success. Build on success until it is easy to repeat and yields you consistent results. Consistency is a form of mastery!

Pattern 1 and 2

Practice the right hand alone patterns below on open strings initially. The thumb (p) should be lightly positioned on the third string. There are two right-hand finger patterns

(1) i - m - i - m pattern on strings two and one respectively, and
(4) m-i-m-i pattern on strings one and two respectively.

　　　　Pattern 1　　　　　　　Pattern 2

String 1		m		m
String 2	i		i	

String 1	m		m	
String 2		i		i

Prelude: Melodic Variety in Seventh Position

The Prelude consists of four two-note chord shapes. By choosing the left-hand finger you can create melodic variety while you practice mastering alternating arpeggiated pattern on the first and second string. **The fingered notes are in seventh position**; that is, the first finger is positioned behind the seventh fret, the second finger behind fret eight, and the fourth finger behind fret ten. Practice the fingering with your left hand before putting the two hands together. Try varied combinations before putting the right and left hand together.

Prelude
(Position Seven)

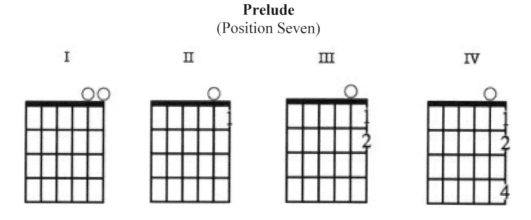

Jacob's Ladder

This simple piece from lesson 3 is in first position. The string numbers refer to frets: "0" is open string; "2" is fret 2. Fingered notes may be played with one or two fingers.

	i	m	i	m	i	m	i	m	i	m	i	m	i	m	i
String 1		0		2	3	2	0		3		2				
String 2	0		0					0		0		0	0	0	

	m	i	m	i	m	i	m	i	m	i	m	i	m	i
String 1		0		2	3	2	0		3	2	0			
String 2			0					0				0	0	0

Lesson 3 Practice Calendar

Three Goals:

(1) Review of principles of music notation, particularly as they apply to rhythm, simple quadruple meter, and strumming rhythms.

(2) Master chords the Em and C while strumming common-time rhythm patterns.

(3) Establish foundation arpeggio technique using free stroke with fingers i and m.

	Sunday	Monday	Tuesday	Wednesday	Thursday	Friday	Saturday
Scales							
Chords							
Arpeggio							
Strum							
New Songs							
Old Songs							

Practice - minimum of 30 minutes per day

Scales: 5 minutes per day
Left exercise two and three

Play each tone twice alternating right-hand fingering; e.g., i - m - i m.

Right hand two note arpeggio patterns: 5 minutes per day
 (1) Etude - Seventh position "i - m - i - m" and "m - i - m - i".

Chord changes - 5 minutes per day
  (1) Synchronized movement -
    (a) two fingers move in parallel direction and arrive at the same
    (b) two fingers move in contrary direction and arrive at the same
  (2) Legato - connected harmonic changes
  (3) Coordinated chord changes with strum or picking

Strum Patterns - 5 minutes
  (1) Two patterns a day
  (2) Accurate rhythm of the strum with index finger
  (3) Strike correct number of strings
  (4) Aim for a full down strum, and light up strung

Song repertoire - 10 minutes
  (1) 5 minutes on new pieces (Quiet Desperation and Prelude).
  (2) 5 minutes on learned repertoire (Impromptu 1-3, Jacob's Ladder).

Lesson 4: Introducing Four Notes in First Position 1

The diagram below represents first three frets (first position) on the fretboard. The zeros above represent the six open strings. The names of the three open bass strings (six, five, four respectively) are E, A, and D; The treble open strings G, B, and E are the third, second, and first string respectively.

The thumb of the left hand should be positioned behind fret 2. Position finger one behind fret 1, finger two behind fret two, and fingers three and four behind fret three. The fingers should be curved. The fingertip of each digit should be perpendicular to the fretboard. The first finger is used for the notes C and F. The fourth finger is used for the notes D and G. The fourth finger is recommended for D and G because distance from frets 7 - 10 in position 7 is roughly the same distance as frets 1 - 3 in first position. Using the fourth finger helps strengthen this comparatively weaker digit. Advancing the coordination and use of the fourth finger also helps prepare the left hand for advanced two-voice textures.

Position 1

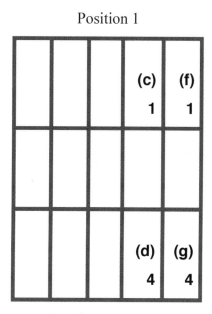

Begin by practicing fingering the four tones in ascending order (C - D - F - G) and in descending order (G - F - D - C). Strike each tone twice alternating between the index ("i") and middle ("m") finger. Moving from string to string will be the most challenging because it involves a simultaneous string position adjustment for both hands.

It may be helpful to practice each hand separately before practicing them together. Beginning with the right hand, strike the first string twice and the second string twice with the i and m fingers. Remember to move the thumb along with the hand when you move from string one to string two. Repeat this transition movement four times. Then add the left and fingering (1and 4). Be creative, change the finger patterns.

16-Bar Blues in G

This following piece uses six notes in position 1. This introductory piece is a 16-bar blues piece in first position. Notes on the third fret string one and two should be played with both first and fourth finger positioned on frets one and three respectively. Play the note on the third fret of string three with the third finger only. This note is the "blues note" of the piece.

Right-hand fingering should alternate between "i" and "m". You may use rest-stroke on the melody. For directions follow direction on https://youtu.be/-s8YunW_Jc . While you play the notes say the letter names of each tone with the intent to imprint and remember the name of each fingered note. Each measure has two tones. Initially hold each tone for two beats (two taps of the foot: down up, down up). Allow four beats of silence (rest) in the fourth bar of line one, two, and four. In time, you may wish to shorten the time value of each note to one beat, making the piece sound like it is at a faster tempo. This piece may be practiced along with an accompanying audio recording. A chordal accompaniment for this song may be found on YouTube: https://youtu.be/SYeT1lHqYH0 .

16-Bar Blues

	Frets	Frets	Frets	Frets
String 1	3 (finger 4) 1			Rest
String 2		3 (finger 4) 1		Rest
String 3			3 0	Rest
Note names	G F	D C	B-flat G	

	Frets	Frets	Frets	Frets
String 1	3 (finger 4) 1			Rest
String 2		3 (finger 4) 1		Rest
String 3			3 0	Rest

	Frets	Frets	Frets	Frets
String 1	3 1		3 1	
String 2		3 1		3 1
String 3				

	Frets	Frets	Frets	Frets
String 1	3 (finger 4) 1			Rest
String 2		3 (finger 4) 1		Rest
String 3			3 0	Rest

Two Chords: G7 and C

The accompanying chords to 16-Bar Blues oscillates between the chords G7 and C. Fingering the G7 chord place the third finger behind fret 3 of the sixth string, the second finger behind the second fret of the fifth string, and the first finger behind the first fret of the first string. Strum down across strings 6, 5, 4, 3, and 2; do not strike string one.

To finger the C chord move the third and second finger over one string, to strings five and four respectively. Additionally, the first finger is positioned behind the first fret of the second string. Strum down across five strings 5, 4, 3, 2, and 1; do not strike the sixth string.

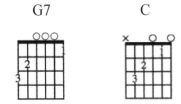

The rhythm of each measure below uses two quarter notes and half note. The bottom number of the time signature indicates a quarter note equals one beat and the half note two beats. Each measure, as indicated by the top number of the time signature, contains four beats. The direction of each strum is down with each half note strum sustaining for two full beats. Counting longer held notes requires both patience and precision. The Beatle song "Paperback Writer" uses G7 & C, play with John, Paul, George, and Ringo: https://youtu.be/xmVwo2DxkGg .

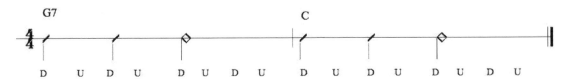

Strumming Rhythms Using Quarter, Half, and Whole Notes

The note types below are whole notes, half notes, and quarter notes. The time signature is 4/4 time; four beats per bar with a quarter note equaling one beat. The note type in the first measure is a whole note with the value of four beats. There are four half notes in measures three and four; each half note receives two beats. The note types in the following two lines contain a mixture of quarter notes and half notes; each measure equals four beats.

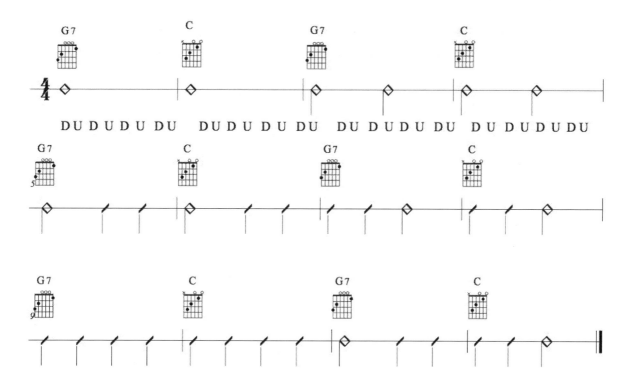

Practice Strategy to Improve Chord Changes

The above mentioned two chords are central chords found in the key of C. The shape of these two chords are similar. Changing to from C to G7 requires moving the third and second finger to the sixth and fifth string respectively while moving the first finger to string one fret 1. One may employ a number of approaches to teaching your fingers to move and arrive simultaneously.

Parallel Movement

The diagonal shape of the third and second fingering is a major third, three semitones (frets). This shape is common to many major chords. Repeatedly moving this shape in parallel movement from string to string helps imprint this chord shape. Begin on the first and second string third and second finger and slowly move the fingers together from string to string maintaining the same shape. This method of practice can also be applied to the chord forms below, moving the third and second fingers back and forth from strings five and four to strings six and five respectively.

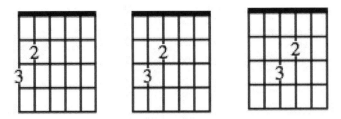

Contrary Movement

The diagonal shape of the third and first finger of the C chord is an octave, while the shape of the second and first finger is a minor sixth. Moving from the C chord to the G7th chord the third and second fingers are moving in a contrary direction to the first finger. The practice of fingers moving in a contrary direction is common. Use a drill exercise to train your fingers to move apart.

Begin by placing the second and first fingers on strings four and second strings respectively. Then lift and simultaneously move the fingers apart one string landing on the fifth and first string; after which, lift and move the fingers together back to the original position.

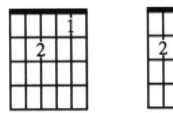

Do the same drill routine focusing on the third and first finger. Moving the third and first fingers on strings five and two respectively to strings six and one respectively. When you have command of these two-finger movements you will ready to training all three fingers to lift and shift to the next chord shape.

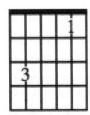 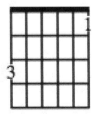

C and G7 Chords with Simple Half-Note Strum

The C and G7 chords may be found in many popular songs. Hank Williams' classic song Jambalaya uses the chord progression below. Singing and strumming a song is complicated because the singer-player is navigating three independent skills: making smooth chord changes, creating a precise rhythm strum, and singing the song. Using the simple half-note strum below may help provide you time to juggle these three skills simultaneously. Play with Hank: https://youtu.be/R7WZZIzTU9A

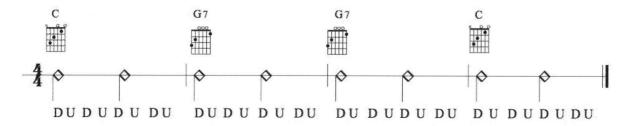

Using an Eighth-note Strum Pattern

When you are able to move and position the fingers simultaneously switching from C to G7, you may add more rhythmically active strum pattern such as the one below. Use the right index finger along with the hand to move down and up in a synchronized manner with the foot. Rock your body with the beat to experience the sensation of the downbeat and upbeat. The down strum on the first beat each measure should include all the chord tones; that is, strings five, four, three two, and one for the C chord. Strum all six strings for the G7 chord. Only the top two strings should be struck by the index finger on the upbeat (when the foot is at its apex).

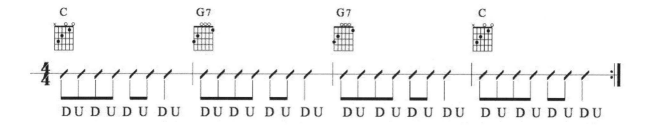

Three-Finger Arpeggio Pattern

The following two arpeggio picking patterns adds the ring finger (a) to the two-finger pattern previously learned. Each finger is assigned a string: the index (i) finger strikes string three, the middle (m) finger string two, and the ring finger (a) string one. Place the thumb (p) gently on the fourth string to help position and stabilize the hand position. Angle the position of the top knuckles so the top knuckle of digit is over the string it is assigned to strike.

Pattern 1				**Pattern 2**		

String 1		a
String 2	m	
String 3	i	

String 1	a	
String 2		m
String 3		i

Play each pattern four times. To avoid rushing, tap your foot once for the first two notes, hold the third note for two beats.

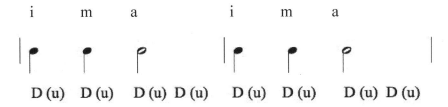

Chord Forms

The chord forms below mat be used in the following arpeggiated piece Wind Chimes. Three of the four chord forms have the same (minor third) shape on the fingerboard. The third chord (C) is has a different (major third) shape. Begin by practice the chord shapes up and down the fingerboard. When you slide up or down the fingerboard the space between the fingers changes. The distance between frets is smaller as you move up the fingerboard the distance, and larger when you move down the fingerboard.

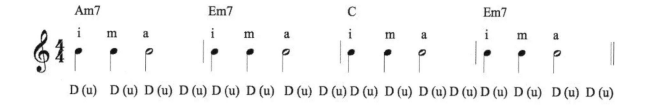

Wind Chimes

Wind Chimes is a delicate instrumental piece which uses the same arpeggio pattern and chords above. After you feel comfortable with the chords and the arpeggio pattern, experiment with different chord combinations.

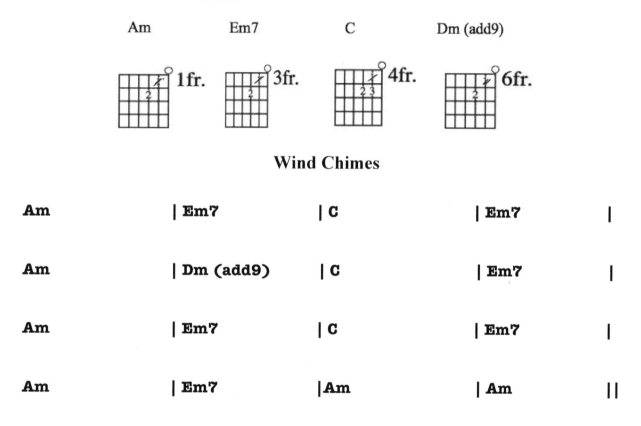

Wind Chimes

Am		Em7		C		Em7	
Am		Dm (add9)		C		Em7	
Am		Em7		C		Em7	
Am		Em7		Am		Am	‖

Lesson 4 Practice Calendar

Three Goals:

(1) To continue to improve control and skill fingering individual notes on strings one and two.

(2) To improve the quality and rhythmic precision of strumming chords, and

establish solid right-hand positioning and execution of movement of the arpeggio technique.

(3) Learn to play arpeggio on the open treble strings using fingers i, m, a. Try playing the pattern while fingering a lovely movable chord form.

	Sunday	Monday	Tuesday	Wednesday	Thursday	Friday	Saturday
Scales							
Chords							
Arpeggio							
Strum							
New Songs							
Old Songs							

Practice - minimum of 30 minutes per day

Scales: 5 minute per day
    a. Left exercise two and three
    b. Play each tone twice alternating right-hand fingering; e.g., i - m - i m.

Right hand two note arpeggio patterns: 5 minutes per day
(1) Etude - Seventh position "i - m - i - m" and "m - i - m - i".

Chord changes - 5 minutes per day
(1) C & G7 chords Synchronized movement -
    (a) two fingers move in parallel direction and arrive at the same
    (b) two fingers move in contrary direction and arrive at the same
(2) Legato - connected harmonic changes
(3) Coordinated chord changes with strum or picking

Strum Patterns - 5 minutes
(1) Two patterns a day
(2) Accurate rhythm of the strum with index finger
(3) Strike correct number of strings
(4) Aim for a full down strum, and light up strung

Song repertoire - 10 minutes
(1) 5 minutes on new pieces: (Wind Chimes, Jambalaya & Paperback Writer).
(2) 5 minutes review Quiet Desperation (previous week).

Lesson 5: Reading Notes in Position 1

As covered in the previous lesson, the diagram below represents the first three frets (first position) on the guitar fretboard. The zeros above represent the six open strings. The names of the three open bass strings (six, five, four respectively) are E, A, and D. The treble open strings G, B, and E are the third, second, and first string respectively.

The thumb of the left hand should be positioned behind fret 2. The first finger is used for the notes C and F. The fourth finger is used for the notes D and G.

Notes in Position 1

			(c)	(f)
			1	1
			(d)	(g)
			4	4

Five-line Notation and Treble (G) Clef

The written music notation below identifies specific musical tones on the staff. The G clef is one of three clefs used to accommodate the tessitura ("vocal range") of individual voices and instruments, in this case the guitar. This clef establishes the note "G" as the second to the bottom line.

```
        String 2              String 1
Name:  C      D         F       G
Fret   1      3         1       3
```

The time signature, common time, is the same as 4/4 time. The top number establishes each measure represents a time frame of four beats. The lower number identifies a quarter note representing one beat. The four tones in the two measures are half notes; each note has a duration of two beats. Last lesson you practiced playing these notes in sequence: C, D, F, G and G, F, D, C; and you learned to play the song 16-bar Blues. This lesson you will learn to read (identify and play) these notes in a song.

In the previous four lessons your primary focus was developing fundamental physical skills to play the guitar. By now you should be able to set both hands in position. Ideally when playing exercises or tunes your left-hand fingers should be even with the frets. Pressing down behind the fret with your fingertip, each finger digit should move independently and remain in position. The right-hand fingers should be relaxed above the strings. The execution of each struck note should result in the finger extending toward the string, touching the string with the fingertip (nail and flesh), follow through down and across the string, ending with the release and return of the finger to its starting position. In reality, you have not yet achieved complete mastery of this skill. It is likely you will find as you concentrate on one hand, the other hand's position is compromised. This is not surprising given the number of things you have to concentrate at one time. Some isolated practice on each hand to train your hands may be helpful.

Two New Chords: G and D

The two chords below, G and D, are related chords in the Keys of G and D. In the key of G, the G chord is the tonic (I) chord, and the D chord is the dominant (V) chord). Changing from this fingering of the chords G to D, the note D (string four open, string two fret three) are common chord tones. The third finger does not need to move when changing from G to D or vice versa. When practicing the chord change G to D visual the second finger as leading the first finger. Practice the movement slowly four times.

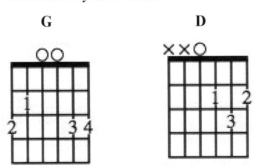

Strumming a Syncopated Rhythm

Syncopation that occurs on the upbeat adds an element of surprise and rhythmic excitement. The rhythmic strum in the first measure below employs an off-beat syncopated rhythms; strums which are occur on successive upbeats. Synchronizing the movement of your right hand with your foot down and up strike the strings in accordance to the rhythmic duration of the note. Beats one and four, the hand strums (down) on the down beat. On beat two the hand strums the strings (down and up) on the downbeat and upbeat. Beat three, the downward movement hand does not strike the strings on the down beat, only (up) on the upbeat. Practice the moving the body to and fro, the foot up and down, while saying the words aloud down and up. Practice playing this rhythm four times.

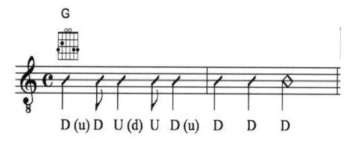

Northwest Moonlight is a rhythm piece using the syncopated strum above. Achieving smooth chord changes will likely require isolating the left hand. Remember the third finger may stay fixed on the third fret of the second string when changing back and forth from the G to D chords. Practice the moving the second and first fingers together. When moving from G to D and D to G let the second finger lead the first. Work to synchronize the movement so the fingers move and arrive together.

Northwest Moonlight

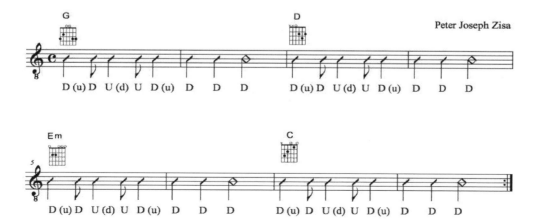

The Importance of Know How

The skill factor of playing a musical instrument corresponds to a musician's level of **know how**. Skill development is a process of training the mind and the body to accomplish a musical task with precision, consistency, and economy of movement. Developing musical skill is the process of learning how to apply technical skills to affect the listening experience. Mastery of an instrument is manifest when the musician no longer has to consciously calculate every action; when the musician's creative and expressive intent is spontaneously and naturally achieved.

Reading Music Notation: Knowing What & When

Learning to play a new piece of music requires knowing **what** to play, **when** to play, and **how** to play the notes. Knowing **what and when** to play is information provided by the music notation. The fingered pitches (**what** component) on the guitar is executed by the left hand; the timing (**when** component) is executed by the right hand. Coordinating what and when to play simultaneously on guitar is difficult to achieve at first sight because the physical dynamic of creating a tone involves two distinct and unrelated techniques. On piano, in contrast, tone and execution occur simultaneously when the key is pushed.

On guitar the location of the fingered tone and timing of the coordinated skills to execute the tone need to be perfectly synchronized between both hands to create a connected (legato) result. The skill (know how) factor can sometimes complicate and interfere with one's mental ability to execute these skills simultaneously. For this reason, it may be helpful to devote individual attention to developing each of these reading skills separately; practicing the right and left hand separately. The following sequence learning activities (practice methods) represent a strategy toward success.

Begin by focusing on **what** to play one or two measures at a time. Read and say the names of the notes aloud. When you can identify and say notes effortlessly, try playing each note in order. As you learn the sequence of the tones (what to play) be sure to observe and control how (hand position, fingering) you are playing the notes. Skill development is related to hand position, fingering, and the quality of execution. Skill is your know-how ability (precision, accuracy, speed, dynamics, and tone production) to play.

Learning **when** to play the notes can be the most difficult task to execute accurately. Simplifying the demands on the left hand is a helpful strategy. Finger a full chord such as the Em or Cmaj7 chord and practice the rhythm as a repeated strum pattern. Remember to tap your foot and gently move your body to the pulse of the music as you accurately conceive and feel the rhythm.

After you have the sequence of tones and rhythm secure, you are ready to put it all together. Begin slowly. Provide enough time between notes to accurately execute both pitch and rhythm. After running through the two measure a few times, assess how you did. Did you play all the right tones, using the desired fingering and positioning precisely? If not, which part was lacking? Does one of the three parts of reading and playing the notes on the page (what, how, when) need individual attention? When you are able to play through the measure correctly, repeat the activity four times to help imprint what you learned in your memory.

Scale Practice as a Warm-up

Your warm-up routine should include a review of the exercises and tunes you have learned. Included in that warm up should be a two-minute slow run through the notes you are now working to commit to memory. Play the sequence of the notes up and down. Begin slowly and work over the course of the week to increase your ability to transition smoothly and more quickly from note to note. Remember to alternate the right-hand fingering using various two-finger patterns.

Learning Your A, B, Cs

The following song is organized into a series of two-bar patterns. The purpose of the tuneful song is to help you practice note reading. **First** read and say the names of the notes aloud. Once you are familiar with **what to play**, play the sequence of notes while focusing on **how to** maintain good hand position and finger execution. Last step, focus on **when** to play the tones. Finger an E-minor or C chord and strum the rhythm of the tune. Strum down on the down beats, and strum up on the up-beats. After you have learned each of the two-bar units (playing each four times), then begin to connect the four pieces into a cohesive melody.

Learning Your A, B, Cs

Andaante (slow tempo)

Peter Jospeh Zisa

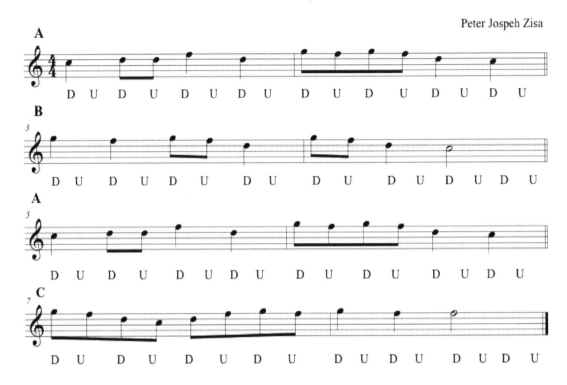

Gold Fish & Syncopated Rhythms

The melody of the piece below uses the four notes in position one: G, F, D, and C. The rhythm of the piece is composed of quarter notes and eighth notes. Using the same practice strategy above, begin by focusing on two measures at a time. First learn **what** the notes are, say the note names aloud. Picture **what** string and fret they are on; visualize **what** fingers you will use to play them. Observe and correct as necessary **how** you play the notes. Be careful about the fingering and position of the fingers. Remember to alternate the right-hand fingering.

Notice which measures repeat. For example, measure one and three contain the same notes and rhythms. Measures three and four display the same melodic fingerings but on different strings. The first two bars of the second line are exactly the same as measures nine and ten (first two bars of the third line). Even measures seven and eight are very similar to measures five and six. Recognizing these patterns can shorten your learning time and even help you memorize a piece.

Learning **when** to play the notes can be the most challenging part of reading music. The off-beat syncopated rhythms in measures six, seven and ten require more concentration and effort to execute precisely. Work to coordinate movement of your foot and body to the downward and upward movement of the beat. The letters "D" and "U" below the notes represent the words down and up part of the beat. Consider strumming the rhythm of the melody to the chord above the melody (or an easier chord if you prefer). Instrumental accompaniment is https://youtu.be/SCQ47e9scMM .

Lesson 5 Practice Calendar

Three Goals:

(1) To read four fingered notes on strings two and one.

(2) To learn chords G and D.

(3) Right hand:

(a) To continue to improve the quality and rhythmic precision of strumming.

(b) To continue to establish solid right hand positioning and execution of the arpeggio technique using fingers i, m, a.

	Sunday	Monday	Tuesday	Wednesday	Thursday	Friday	Saturday
Scales							
Chords							
Arpeggio							
Strum							
New Songs							
Old Songs							

Practice - minimum of 30 minutes per day

Scales: 5 minute per day

(1) Left exercise two and three
(2) Play four-tone scale four times a day alternating right-hand fingering: i - m - i m.

Right hand two note arpeggio patterns: 5 minutes per day

(1) Etude - Seventh position "i - m - i - m" and "m - i - m -i".

Chord changes - 5 minutes per day

(1) Chords G and D
(2) Legato - connected harmonic changes
(3) Coordinated chord changes with strum or picking

Strum Patterns - 5 minutes

(1) Two patterns a day
(2) Accurate rhythm of the strum with index finger
(3) Strike correct number of strings
(4) Aim for a full down strum, and light up strung

Song repertoire - 10 minutes

(1) 5 minutes on new piece (Goldfish & ABC song),
(2) 5-minute review: Wind Chimes, Jambalaya & Paperback Writer, Quiet Desperation.

Lesson 6: Filling in the Gaps

The diagram below represents the first three frets (first position) of the guitar fretboard. The thumb of the left hand should be positioned behind fret 2. The first finger is used for the notes C and F. The fourth finger is used for the notes D and G. The right-hand thumb should be placed two strings above the struck string: string five to strike the third string, string four for the second, and string three for the first. Lesson six includes the open-string notes B and E on string 2 and 1 respectively.

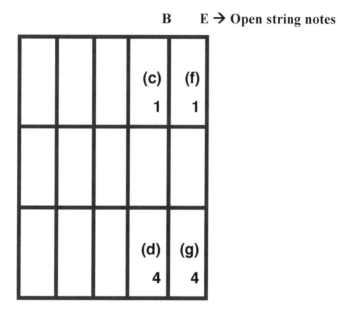

The scale below includes all six notes on the second and first string. The scale begins on the note C goes down a semitone to B and then ascends stepwise to the note G on string one. It is difficult to execute all the notes accurately and in good form the first time. Allow more time between notes to better control the result, it is helpful to practice new music at half tempo. Playing at half tempo doubles the time value of all the notes. Each quarter note in the scale would receive two beats at half tempo.

Notes on String 1 & 2

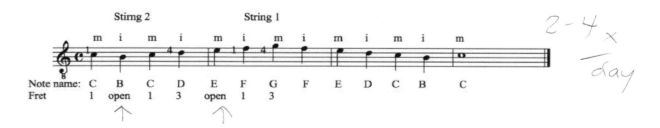

2-4 x day

Sight-Reading

As your skill become more refined and consistent, you will find you can rely on guitar skills and focus your attention on the music in front of you. How will you know you have reached that point? When playing the guitar becomes more "second nature". Your hand will naturally go into position, when fingers remain in position, when you begin to anticipate the melodic and harmonic patterns you learned and committed to memory. Remember, any time you learn something new, however, there will be a learning period.

The piece below uses the four of the six notes you have learned. With this information, you can identify which notes are not included in this piece by looking for notes that you can easily see do not move up or down the musical alphabet stepwise. Begin by looking at measure one for notes that move from line to line or space to space. When notes move from line to line or space to space a note (letter) has been skipped. Which notes were skipped? Which two notes moved stepwise? You have now identified all the notes used in this piece.

Slowly at half tempo play these four notes in measure one four times. How difficult is it to remember and identify the open notes? Watch your left hand the fourth time. What new difficulty did you experience? Did your first finger point away from the fingerboard when you played D or G? If so, try putting both the first and fourth finger down on the same string when playing D or G. It will take some learning time to recognize the open string notes and make this new practice second nature.

Haiku ✓

Peter Joseph Zisa

(1) **What to play:** say the note names in two bar units four times.

(2) **How to play:** Alternate right hand fingering. Finger both first (fret 1) and fourth finger (fret 3) when playing notes D and G.

(3) **When** to play: keep a steady beat, hold half notes for two beats.

E-Z Does It

E-Z Does It is a 12-bar Blues-style piece. Examine the first measure. Do you notice any similarities to the previous piece? If you do, examine the next three measures to see if this pattern continues. Begin by focusing on one or two measures. Read and say the names of the notes aloud four times. After you can identify **what** to play, slowly play each note in order. As you learn the sequence of the tones (what to play) observe and control **how** (hand position, fingering) you playing the notes. The most difficult factor will be the right-hand fingering. Learning **when** to play the notes may prove difficult if you are still working on memorizing the sequence of tones. Try practicing the rhythm as a strum, possibly fingering the E7 chord. Another strategy would be to practice the piece at half tempo; eighth notes would equal one beat and quarter notes two. The rhythm in measure 3, 4, 7, 8, and 12 includes a dotted quarter note, which has the time value of three eighth notes (1 and a half beats).

Performance practice sometimes is different from the written rhythmic notation. Coupled eighth notes in the blues style has a characteristic "swing". The first note receives twice the value of the second. If we divide the beat into three parts and assign each part a syllable it would sound like the name: JO-se-phine. The first eighth note would last for JO-se, and the second eighth note would occur on "phine". Try using the word Josephine to feel the stylistic difference.

Olé

Olé is a Spanish Andalusian flamenco style piece. The melody is reminiscent of the famous piece Malagueña. Malagueña is one of the Fandango dances from the province of Málaga. The melody of the first line is in stepwise motion. The tempo of the piece, which begins slowly (Andante) should accelerate with each repetition until it reaches a fast tempo (Allegro).

The second half of the piece is rhythmically syncopated. The rhythmic figure is the same as the cake-walk rhythm found in Goldfish melody. You may enjoy practicing this rhythm by strumming the chords E and **F***. The **F*chord,** which is fingered the same as the E chord, is in second position; that is, the first finger is positioned on string 3 fret two, the second and third finger are fingered on the third fret on strings five and four respectively. See the instructional video: https://youtu.be/wM5YTFpnO14 .

Arpeggio: Adding the Thumb (" P")

Pollex (pulgar, Spanish), AKA the Thumb.

The most flexible digit of the right hand is the thumb. The thumb most commonly is used to strike the bass strings: strings 4, 5, and 6. "P" is an acrostic letter for the Latin word pollex (Latin), or Spanish word pulgar, for the thumb.

(1) Position the hand with the index and middle finger on the second and first string respectively and the top knuckles forward over the first two strings.

(2)   Reach back and place the thumb on string four.

(3) The middle of the thumb (nail) should be in direct contact with the string.

(4) Pull the finger across the fourth until it rests on string three.

   (a) The manner the stroke is accomplished begins from the middle (nail) of the thumb with the last contact with the string occurring on the left corner of the thumb (nail).

(5) After the thumb comes to a "rest" on string three release the thumb and direct to return to its original position above the fourth string.

Without moving the hand extend the thumb to the fifth string. Repeat the same five-step procedure. The hand should remain in the same position when striking the fourth, fifth, or sixth string with the thumb. Play the open fourth, fifth, and sixth string. Watch and maintain the position of the hand. While the thumb has the movement flexibility enough to reach each of the three bass strings, the hand will be naturally inclined to move towards the bass string. Maintaining the position essential for the fingers (i, m, and a) to be in position to strike the treble strings. The goal is to achieving control of the thumb stroke and hand position. The next step is to combine the free stroke (using "i", "m", and "a") with the thumb.

Arpeggio Pattern 1 and 2

Pattern 1 and 2 combine the thumb stroke on string 4 with "i" and "m" on the second and first string respectively.

(1) Use rest stroke (apoyando) to strike the fourth string with the thumb.

   (a) The fingers ("i" and "m") should be above strings two and one. (b) The hand should be relaxed and fixed in its position.

(2) Leave the thumb lightly *resting* on string three.

   Strike second and first string free stroke (tirando) with the i and m fingers.

   (a) The fingers ("i" and "m") should return to a prepared position after each stroke.

Pattern 1

String 1			m	
String 2		i		i
String 4	P			

Pattern 2

String 1		m		m
String 2			i	
String 4	P			

Preludio Del Amore

The following piece, Preludio Del Amore, may be played using pattern 1 or 2. The melody of the piece is entirely on the fourth string. The numbers in the boxes indicate the fret of fingered melody tones. You are encouraged to use only the second finger to play the melodic tones. This will cause you to make constant position changes. After you memorize and feel comfortable playing the arpeggio pattern and making all the position shifts, try playing the piece without watching your left hand. Playing the piece without looking at your hands is another level of mastery. See instructional video 14 and practice video 15.

Preludio Del Amore Practice Steps

Step 1

    (1) Use rest stroke (apoyando) to strike the fourth string with the thumb.

        (a) Follow through until thumb "rests" on string three.

    (2) The fingers ("i" and "m") should be above strings two and one.

        (a) Use free stroke (tirando) on strings two and one.

    (3) Play the melody (the bass notes) louder than top treble strings.

    (4) Use pattern one (p-i-m-i) and pattern two (p-m-i-m).

    (5) Strum an E minor chord at the end.

    (6) Experiment creating other melodies using the notes.

Preludio Del Amore

	p i m i	p i m i	p i m i	p i m i	p i m i	p i m i	p i m i	p i m i
String 4	2	4	5	4	2	5	7	7
String 4	2	4	5	4	2	0	2	2
String 4	9	12	10	9	7	5	9	9
String 4	2	4	5	4	2	0	2	2

Step 2

(1) Strum E minor chord as final chord

(2) Emphasize bass melody

(3) Dynamically shape bass melody

(4) Use alternative picking patterns: P m i m

(5) Experiment creating and adding new melodic phrases

Step 3 - Two additional Arpgeggio Patterns:

The additional arpeggio patterns below include the "a" (ring) finger. While the thumb is still assigned string 4, the index, middle, and ring fingers strike strings 3, 2, and 1 respectively. All fingers strike the strings in a free stroke (tirando) manner. Points of difficulty are:

    (1) Keeping the hand in position over the treble strings,

    (2) Keeping the hand relaxed in a fixed position throughout,

(3) Dynamically striking the bass melody louder (mf - F) than the accompanying open-string tones.

Meditation

Pima

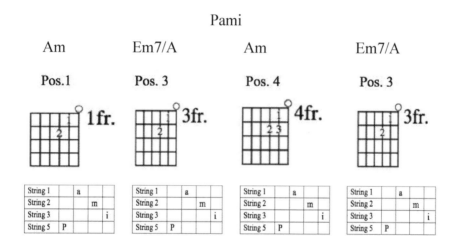

Pami

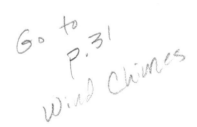

Lesson 6 Practice Calendar

Two Goals:

(1) Learn read six notes on strings one and two in Position 1 (including open strings).

(2) Learn to play arpeggio including the thumb. Two arpeggio patterns: P-i-m-i and P-m-i-m.

	Sunday	Monday	Tuesday	Wednesday	Thursday	Friday	Saturday
Scales							
Chords							
Arpeggio							
Strum							
New Songs							
Old Songs							

Practice - minimum of 30 minutes per day

Scales: 5 minutes per day
a. Left exercise two and three

b. Play six-note scale in position one; alternate right-hand fingering: i - m - i m.

Right hand two note arpeggio patterns: 5 minutes per day
(1) P- i - m - i and P - m - i m arpeggio patterns. **Preludio Del Amore**

Chord changes - 5 minutes per day
(1) Synchronized movement -

(a) two fingers move in parallel direction and arrive at the same

(b) two fingers move in contrary direction and arrive at the same

(2) Legato - connected harmonic changes

(3) Coordinated chord changes with strum or picking

Strum Patterns - 5 minutes
(1) Two patterns a day

(2) Accurate rhythm of the strum with index finger

(3) Strike correct number of strings

(4) Aim for a full down strum, and light up strung

Song repertoire - 10 minutes
(1) 5 minutes on new melody pieces: Song of choice: Haiku, E-Z Blues, or Olé.

(2) 5 minutes on new arpeggiated pieces: Preludio Del Amore and Meditation.

Lesson 7: Chords and Harmony

This lesson focuses on harmony and melody as related to three chords C, Am, and G7. A brief lesson in music theory will explain how chords are harmonically constructed; how they are related and how they are different from each other. Strumming is simply a rhythmic presentation of harmony on guitar. You will learn a six rhythmic strum patterns which you may use in accompanying your singing. Compare the individual chord (harmonic) tones of these chords and how they are represented in a scale and key of a song. Lastly, experiment playing with these tones and create a tune that is related to the harmony and visa-versa.

Chords and Harmony

A chord is a group of tones sounding together. In traditional western harmony chords are described as triads. The tones of a triad consist of three tones (a third) apart from each other. The note E is three notes apart from C (c-d-e), and the note G is three notes apart from E (e-f-g). The chord C is built on the note "C"; the two other tones of a C chord are "e" and "g". The name of a chord represents the scale tones of the chord it is built above. A C chord is chord built on the first tone of a C scale; an A chord is built on the sixth scale degree of a C scale.

Major and Minor chords

The descriptive quality of chords is described as major and minor. "Am" is an "A" minor chord (a-c-e). If the letter name of a chord does not have a small *m*, it is a *major* chord. The "C" chord below is major chord. The difference between major and minor chords is determined by the middle voice of the triad. The major third (distance between c and e for example) is a half a step (one fret) larger than its corresponding minor third (distance between c and e-flat). If the middle voice has a distance of three frets (half steps), as it is from "a" to "c", it is a minor third (minor chord). If the middle voice is four frets away, as it is from "c" to "e", it is a major third (major chord). Examine and compare the distance of C to E and A to C.

E	A	D	G	B	E
				C	(F)
			A		
				(D)	(G)
			(B)		
			C	E	(A)

Because the middle voice of a C major chord is a major third we identify the quality of its sound as major. On the chart below the note *e* is more conveniently located on the open first string. In contrast, because the distance between from A to C is a minor third, we hear the quality of an A-C-E triad as minor. A and C are found on the third and second string respectively. Play and compare these two chords.

C major chord   A minor chord

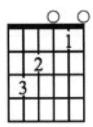 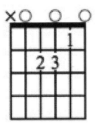

Rhythm Guitar: Chords and Rhythm

    Strumming chords on a guitar is a rhythmic expression of harmony. The fundamental component of rhythm is the beat which may be divided into two parts: the down beat and up-beat. The strum on the first down beat in a measure of music is the fullest, consists of the most chord tones. This is accomplished by strumming all the available chord tones in the fingering. In the case of the Am and C chord, the first strum should include five strings. The down strums on beats 2, 3, and 4 do not necessary include all five strings. The up-beat strum has a brighter thinner tone quality. Achieving this tonal quality is achieved by strumming up on the treble strings (strings 1, 2, and 3).

    Before beginning to strum tap your foot and move your body to the rhythm of the beat. Feel the two parts of the beat, the down beat and up-beat. Coordinate the down strum to the movement of the down beat, and the up strum to the lighter upward movement of the foot and body. Maintain this coordinating movement throughout.

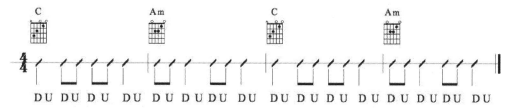

Chord Changes and Common Chord Tones

Chord changes need to be quick to maintain continuously steady pulse. The chords C and Am have two common chord tones: C and E. When practicing changing chords don't lift fingers unnecessarily. In the case of Am and C, only the third finger moves; the first and second finger maintain the same position on the fretboard.

Syncopated Rhythms

The curve connecting line in the strum pattern below is called a tie and indicates the strummed tones are sustained for both rhythm values. There are three strums within the first two beats of measure one and three: Down, up, and up. There is no down strum on beat two. The effect of two up strums is described as a syncopated rhythm. While the guitar is not strummed on the second down beat, the guitarist should continue to tap the foot along and move the hand in downward movement (to feel the down beat).

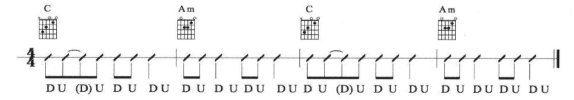

Seventh Chords

Numbers that follow the letter name of a chord represents an additional chord tone and its relative distance from the root of the chord. The number "7" in an Am7 chord represents the tone "G" tone, which is seven tones above the note "A". G7 is a major triad (g-b-d) with the added tone "F"; which is seven tones above "G". G7 is a special chord in the key of C. Because G is five tones above the tonal key center C (C, D, E, F, G), G7 is described as the dominant-seventh chord. The harmonic tension of the tones of the dominant-seventh chord causes the listener to *expect* and *desire* the following chord will resolve to C, the tonal key center. Play, listen and observe how the G7 below first *causes* you to desire resolution from the harmonic tension and *feel* satisfied when you hear C major chord. This is described by music theorists as a "tension-release" relationship between the dominant seventh and tonic chords.

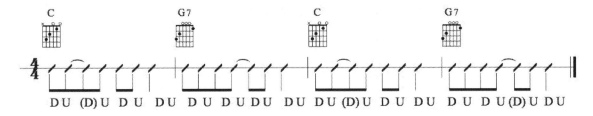

Two Songs to Learn

There are many songs that are built on two chords. The following familiar folk songs represent excellent tunes for your music therapy clinical repertoire. Compare the melody with the chords. **What** are the note names in each two-bar unit? Which melodic notes are harmonic and non-harmonic? Practice the tune and the chords. **How** are your guitar skills developing? Does the left-hand position and fingering should feel more natural to you? Do you have difficulty alternating the right-hand fingering? The right-hand fingering may require extra concentrated effort. When you can change chords smoothly try strumming steady quarter notes (down strokes only) while singing the song. When you can accomplish this comfortably, raise the level of difficulty by strumming steady eighth notes (down and up) while singing.

Mary Had A Little Lamb

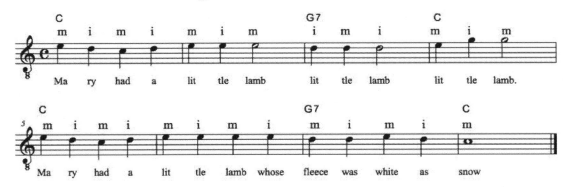

Go Tell Aunt Rhody

Polyrhythmic Difficulties in Singing and Strumming

Singing and strumming the guitar can be difficult at first. This is not surprising if you consider how many things you are trying to manage at the same time: the lyrics, the rhythm and pitch of the melody, the chords and chord changes, and last the strum pattern. Typically, the strum pattern generates a complimentary independent rhythm. When singing and strumming you are generating a polyrhythmic effect.

Choosing the Complimentary Strum

Rhythmically independent strum patterns that includes eighth-notes should generate rhythmic interest and compliment the melody. If the strum pattern is too complex it may confuse the singers and make singing along more difficult. A complimentary strum pattern should help enable the singers to feel more rhythmically connected to melody. Selecting or creating a complimentary strum pattern has two goals: generating interest and making singing easier and more appealing. Consider the following two strum patterns:

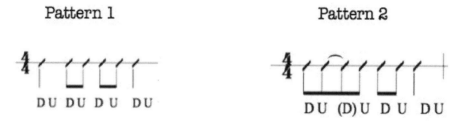

Say aloud the lyrics of Go Tell Aunt Rhody as rhythmically notated below. Placing your left hand across the six strings of the guitar, mute the open string tones of the guitar. Synchronizing the movement of your foot and hand, strum the first pattern repeatedly four times. Begin by tapping your foot and initiating strum pattern for two bars. Then add the lyrics in time! Tricky? It may take a few efforts before you can successfully execute this. Afterwards, turn your attention to Pattern 2. After playing the pattern four times, try adding the lyrics in time. Which pattern was easier to execute? Which pattern do you prefer to sing with? Now try the same to patterns for Mary Had a Little Lamb.

Scales and Melody

A melody is a tuneful sequence of tones. A small melodic unit, a sub-phrase, is commonly two measures in length. Using the six tones you have learned and borrowing from the rhythmic sequence of the two previous songs, compose a simple four-bar tune. Try different melodic combinations. Write down the one(s) you like best.

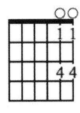

G & A: Two Notes on the Third String

Add two notes on the third-string: G and A, the open and second fret respectively.
Play all eight tones, up and down, as quarter notes holding the last tone as a half note. Do this a minimum of four times; if needed, continue playing the scale until you feel comfortable playing the eight-tone scale.

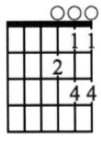

Play the chord tones of a C (C-E-G) and an A minor chord (A-C-E) as scale tones as shown in the diagrams below. Melodic tones which match the chord tones are described as "harmonic tones".

Matching Melodic Tones with Chordal Harmony

Create a four-measure tune to the four-chord progression: C, Am, G7, C. Try matching melodic tones with the harmony. After drawing a treble clef at the beginning of each system write 4/4 for common time. At the beginning of the first measure write C for a C major chord (tones: C-E-G). In measure two write Am for an A minor chord (tones: A-C-E); in measure three write G7 (tones: G-B-D-F) and measure four C. While you may use non-chord tones in your melody, try to use more chord tones. Again, play six tones for each two-measure phrase: five even quarter notes pausing two beats (a half note) on the sixth note. Try different combinations. Write down the tones you like best.

Varying and Expanding the Melodic Possibilities

A melody is a tuneful sequence of tones. Tunes which stimulate our interest create surprising and satisfying combinations. Melodies also represent the voice of the storyteller. The melodic story is complimented and reinforced by *harmony*. Harmonic dissonance contributes to feelings of conflict and resolution. Melodic tones that are the same as the supporting harmony represent harmonic tones. Melodic tones which differ from the harmonic tones are described non-harmonic tones.

The melody of the theme uses mostly harmonic (chord) tones. Because of this, the melody is composed of thirds; i.e., melodic tones that are three notes apart (e.g., C to E, E to G). As it is with walking, it is easier to sing melodies that move stepwise, than melodies that are filled with only skips and large leaps. The three variations that follow are melodic variations that move more stepwise. Variation two contain more strongly dissonant (non-harmonic) tones. The dissonant non-harmonic tones occurring on the strong beats (one and three), are described as appoggiaturas (*sighing tones*). The majority of the non-harmonic tones in Variation 3 move stepwise and are musically described as *passing tones*. At closer examination of the two previous songs, Mary Had a Little Lamb and Aunt Rhody, the melody of both songs use mostly chord tones. Most of the non-harmonic tones in these two songs are passing tones.

Theme & Variations

Peter Joseph Zisa

Lesson 7 Practice Calendar

Two Goals:

(1) Master changes for two new progressions: C -to Am, Am to C;

    Master two chord rhythm strums

(2) Introduction of notes on the third string and eight-note scale

	Sunday	Monday	Tuesday	Wednesday	Thursday	Friday	Saturday
Scales							
Chords							
Arpeggio							
Strum							
New Songs							
Old Songs							

Practice - 30 - 45 minutes per day

Scales: 2 minutes per day (G scale)
    (1) One octave (mixolydian) scale at quarter note pace - four times.
        Play each tone twice to ensure you alternate fingering.

Chord changes - 3 minutes per day
    (1) Synchronized movement - fingers move and arrive at the same
        time - C to Am - Am to C, C to G7, G7 to C, Am to G7.
    (2) Minimum goal: four times for each chord change
        One minute for each until mastered.

Arpeggio Patterns: i-m; i-a, m-a; i-m-a, a-m-i; p-i-m-i, p-m-i-m
    10 minutes per day
    (1) Two patterns a day: quarter note pace - seven times
    (2) Observe and correct position, follow through
    (3) Practice at four different dynamic levels: p, mp, mf, F

Strum Patterns - (none this week) - 10 minutes
    (1) Two patterns a day
    (2) Accurate rhythm of the strum with index finger
    (3) Strike correct number of strings
    (4) Aim for a full down strum, and light up strung

New Songs - 10 - 15 minutes per day
    (1) Mary Had a Little Lamb, Go Tell Aunt Rhody,
        Theme and Variations

Song repertoire - 10 minutes
    Preludio Del Amore -Z Does it, Ole!

Lesson 8: Shapes, Forms, & the Circle of Fifths

Lesson 8 introduces the fingering shape of a sixth. A sixth is an interval (distance) of six notes. The sixth, an inversion of a third, is a part of a chord form. In the process we will examine and add three new chords to your chord vocabulary: Am7, Dm, and E7. The first challenge making legato (quick and smooth) chord changes. Helpful practice strategies will help you master these chord changes. Lastly, the notes G and A on string third will be introduced as part a mixolydian scale with the range of an octave (eight notes).

Moving Sixths

The fingering shape below represents an interval of a sixths (e.g., **E** f g a b **C**). This shape appears in an abundance of chord forms, including the following three chords: Am, Dm, and E7. Mastering the movement of this shape is helpful to making chord changes quickly and smoothly. Practice moving to each of parallel "sixth shape" as shown below. It is essential fingers lift and move together in a simultaneous parallel movement. This skill exercise is best done focusing on the left hand alone.

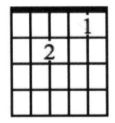 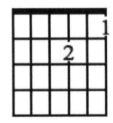 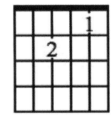 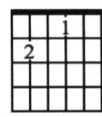

Am7 and Dm chords

Practice strumming the Am7 and Dm chords. Strum the Am7 chord twice. Then quickly move the first and second fingers to the third and first strings respectively. There should be no hesitation or loss of time when switching chords.

The Dm chord has one extra finger to place, the fourth finger on the second string third fret. This may prove to be more difficult to execute in a timely manner. When fingering the Am chord prepare the fourth finger by aligning it over the second string third fret. Then when slowly work on getting the fourth finger in position at the same time as the first and second finger. Synchronizing the movement of all three fingers is the key to achieving a legato (connected) chord change.

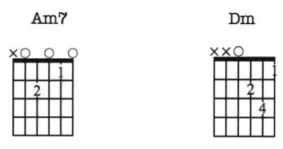

Am to Dm

Moving from Am to Dm is accomplished in much the same way as Am7 to Dm. The only additional complication it the positioning of the third finger when fingering the Am chord. This addition results in nudging the second finger closer to the first fret. When moving to Dm allow the second to be more centered.

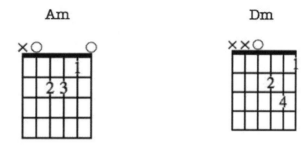

This chord combination appears in many songs. The song "Miss You" by the Rolling Stones uses only Am and Dm. After you are able to skillfully make legato chord changes, consider playing the song "Miss You" along with the Rolling Stones, see https://youtu.be/uetJoJj0M88 .

Am7 and E7 chords

Switching between Am7 and E7 chords should be easier. Strum the Am7 chord twice. Then, moving the first and second finger to the fifth and fourth string respectively, strum the E7 chord twice. Chord changes should be quick and smooth, with no hesitation or loss of time between the chords.

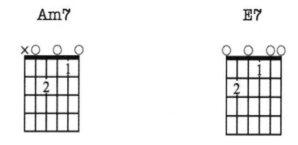

Harmonic Relationship of Using Scale Degrees

The sixth century Greek mathematician Pythagoras discovered measured ratios using a one-string research instrument called the monochord. Pythagoras discovered 2:1 relationship in the pitch we identify as an octave and a 3;2 relationship in producing a tone we identify as fifth. Consequent to this, Pythagoras applied the mathematic ratio (3:2) to develop a tuning system historians call the Pythagorean tuning. This tuning system was modified as "tempered" tuning over the centuries. In the 20th century an equal temperament system was adopted.

The Circle of Fifths Relationship in Harmonic Progression

The Pythagorean tuning system played an important role in the development of western music. Plainchant melodies from the early middle ages (6th century) exhibit a tonal relationship "dominant" tone and "final" tone.

With development of major and minor scales the dominant (V) tonic (I) relationship became central part of the development of harmony. This relationship was pervasive in the development of major and minor keys. Moving up the circle of fifths the sequence of fifths is: C, G, D, A, E, B, F#, and C#. Go down the circle of fifths and the order of flat is manifest.

Composers and music theorists like Jean-Phillipe Rameau (1683-1764) noted the circle of fifths also applied to harmonic relationship of one chord to another. A series of chords following the pattern of the circle fifths has a powerful connection. The I-vi-ii-V7 chord progression is such an example. The chord progression C to Am to Dm to G7 to C (I vi ii V7) represents an example of how the circle fifths commonly appears in songs of old and today.

The three following two-bar strum patterns have three levels of difficulty. The first pattern uses a simple quarter note rhythm. The technical difficulty rests in the different number strings to be strummed for each chord. For the C and A minor five string are struck, for the D minor chord only four strings, and the G7 chord all six strings should sound. Addressing the tonal quality of strum is another factor improve upon. A quick stroke brushing the top of the strings is most desirable. If the arc of the strum is too circular the tonal result will be treble or bass heavy.

The second strum pattern employs combination of simple quarter and eighth note rhythms. The difficulty is adding the light up-stroke strum on the two high treble strings while maintaining the same quality of result on the down strums.

The third two-bar pattern is the most rhythmically complex. In first measure, two consecutive syncopated up-stroke strums occur. Remember to count "down" and "up" aloud keeping the movement your body and arm synchronized. The greater rhythmic complexity of the last two strum patterns may interfere with the smoothness of the chord changes.

Three Strum Patterns: Playing with Heart and Soul

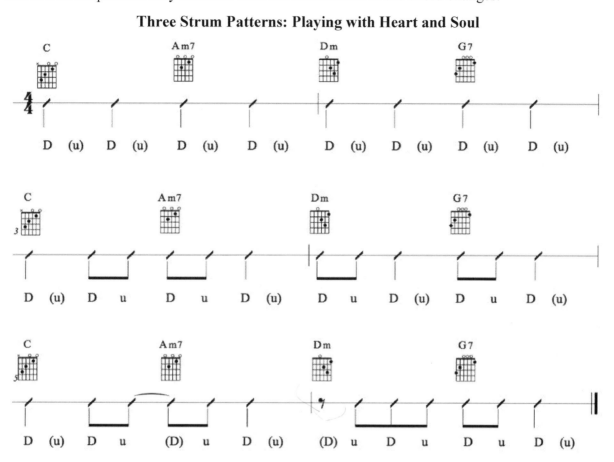

Corresponding Arpeggiated Accompaniment

The arpeggiated accompaniment below should be practiced first as even quarter notes and later as even eighth notes. One of the challenges for the right hand is the changes of bass notes for Dm and G7. A secondary issue may be ensuring all the struck chord tones are clear and sustained.

In 1938 Howard "Hoagy" Carmichael composed the immensely popular song Heart and Soul. The song uses chord progression is I - vi - ii - V7. In 1939 three renditions of the song scored high on the charts (#1, #12, #16). The popularity of the song continued in the 1950s and 1960s. In 2016 the group Train covered this song as "Play the Song". The melody of the song will no doubt be familiar to you. The melody is restricted to the six notes on strings one and two. Play and sing along with Train: https://youtu.be/J5qWnG5RQTk .

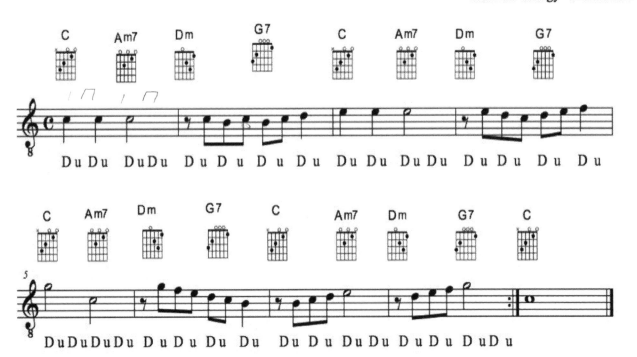

Original Lyrics:

Heart and soul, I fell in love with you.
Heart and soul, the way fools madly do.
Because you held me tight.

The eighth-note rest on beat one followed by three eighth notes in measures 2, 4, 6, 7, and 8 is similar to the last measure of the previous third strum pattern (see below).

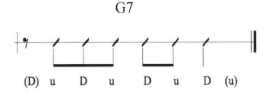

G & A: Two Notes on the Third String

The scale below adds two notes on the third-string: G and A, the open and second fret respectively. Play all eight tones, up and down, as quarter notes holding the last tone as a half note. Play this scale a minimum four times per day. If the scale is difficult, play it slower until you feel comfortable with the scale. This scale is identified as a mixolydian mode.

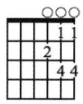

Matching Melodic Tones with Chordal Harmony

Using the C, Am, Dm, and G7 chord progression create your own four-measure tune. Try matching melodic tones with the harmony. After drawing a treble clef at the beginning of each system write 4/4 for common time. At the beginning of the first measure write C for a C major chord (tones: C-E-G). In measure two write Am7 for an A-minor-seventh chord (tones: A-C-E); in measure three write Dm (D-F-A) for D minor chord; and G7 (tones: G-B-D-F) in measure four. While you may use non-chord tones in your melody, try to use more chord tones.

Lesson 8 Practice Calendar

Three Goals:

(1) Master changes for two chord changes: Am -> Dm; Am -> E7

Master changes for two progressions: C -> Am -> Dm -> G7 -> C

(2) Master two chord rhythm strums (Strum and sing Heart and Soul) and arpeggio accompanyment.

(3) Introduction of notes on the third string and eight-note scale

	Sunday	Monday	Tuesday	Wednesday	Thursday	Friday	Saturday
Scales							
Chords							
Arpeggio							
Strum							
New Songs							
Old Songs							

Practice - 30 - 40 minutes per day

Scales: 2 minutes per day (G scale)
    (1) One octave at quarter note (one second) - four times.
    Play each tone twice to ensure you alternate fingering.

Chord changes - 3 minutes per day
    (1) Synchronized movement - fingers move and arrive at the same
        time - Am/Am7 to Dm; Am to E7, Dm to E7, and Dm to G7.
    (2) Four times for each chord change up to minute for each until mastered.

Arpeggio Patterns: P-i-m-i, P-m-i-m; P-i-m-a, P-a-m-i;10 minutes per day
    (1) Two patterns a day: quarter note pace - eight times
    (2) Observe and correct position, follow through
    (3) Practice at four different dynamic levels: p, mp, mf, F
        (a) Practice crescendo (gradually getting louder) and decrescendo

Strum Patterns - 10 minutes
    (1) Two patterns a day
    (2) Accurate rhythm of the strum with index finger
    (3) Strike correct number of strings
    (4) Aim for a full down strum, and light up strung

New Songs - 10 minutes per day
    (1) Miss You, and Heart and Soul (Play the Song, 2016)

Song repertoire - 10 minutes
    (1) Miss you, Heart and Soul, and your own song.
    (2) Preludio Del Amore, E-Z does it, Jambalaya, Mary Had a Little Lamb…

Lesson 9: I - II7 - V7 Vamp

pg. 89-70
Think you can do it!

Lesson 9 adds one new chord D7 along and another popular chord progression: C D7 G7 C (I - II7 - V7 - I). There are numerous popular songs which use this progression. Aura Lee, a popular among both the confederate and union soldiers, is one of them. You may recognize this song as Elvis Presley's song Love Me Tender. You will learn to play the melody and chords to Aura Lee. The melody uses the two new notes on the third string G and A.

C and D7

The chords C (C-E-G) and D7 (D-F#-A-C) have one note in common: the note C. This note is on string two fret one. When changing from the C chord to the D7 do not move or lift the first finger. The second and third finger need to move together toward the treble strings. Allow the third finger to pass the second finger on route to the first string third fret. Watch the second as it follows close behind the third finger.

C

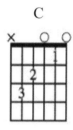

D7

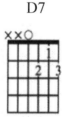

D7 and G7

The chords D7 (D-F#-A-C) and G7 (G-B-D-F) have one note in common: the note D. This note is the open fourth string. D7 is the dominant-seventh chord to G, and G is the dominant-seventh chord to C.

D7

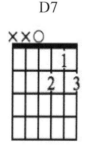

G7

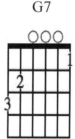

Divide and Conquer

When changing chords from D7 to G7 the second and first fingers move contrary (opposite) direction of the first finger, as do the first and third fingers. It is helpful to isolate these two-finger combinations to better control the accuracy of the movement of these fingers in practice.

Both fingers should move and arrive simultaneously.

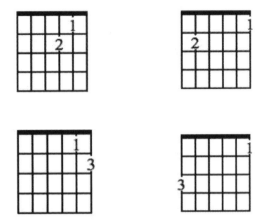

The second and third fingers, in contrast, move in the same direction. Allow the third finger to pass and lead the second finger. Isolating the movement of these fingers in practice may be helpful.

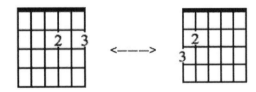

Combining these movements in one simultaneous and synchronized movement is the last step. Begin by visualizing the movement of the fingers: The fingers lift, three passes and leads two toward the bass strings while the first finger positions itself over string 1 fret 1. When the fingers are positioned over the strings and frets, they simultaneously take their position. Practice mentally visualizing this movement before physically doing it. If you need more time to master a two-finger combination, repeat the two-finger movement.

After you have solid control of the chord changes add the strum patterns below:

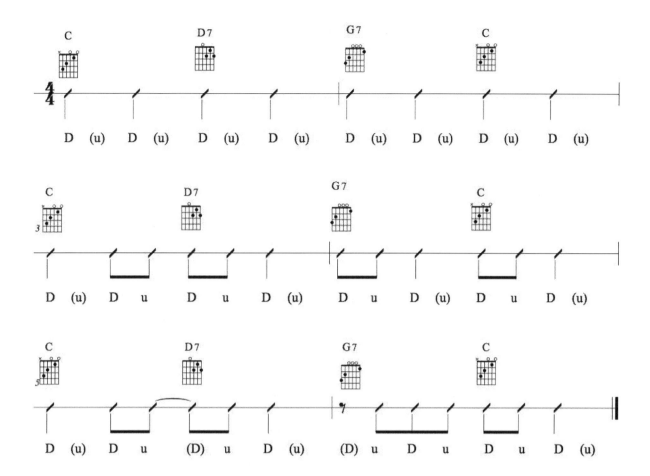

Eight Notes on the First Three Strings

Play all eight tones (g, a, b, c, d, e, f, g) from string 3 open to string 1 fret 3, up and down, as quarter notes holding the last tone as a half note. Use the fourth finger for the notes "d" and "g". Play this scale four times.

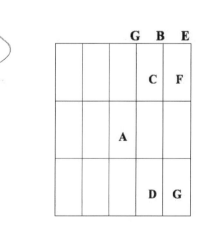

The first two notes of the mixolydian scale below are "G" and "A" on string three, open and fret two respectively. Play the mixolydian scale four times.

Scale: Mixolydian Mode

Line Notes and Space Note

The following four bars are "line notes"; that is, all notes that appear on the lines. Each note skips a tone; therefore, the notes are a third apart: **G** (a) **B** (c) **D** (e) **F**. The notes below are the individual tones of a G dominant-seventh chord. Play the tones of a G7 up and down four times. Think and say the note names as you play them.

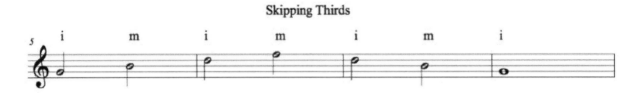

The following four bars are "space notes", notes that appear between the lines. Each note skips a tone; therefore, each note is a third apart: **A** (b) **C** (d) **E** (f) **G**. The notes below are the individual tones of an A minor seventh chord. Play the tones of an Am7 up and down four times. Think and say the note names as you play them.

Old Joe Clarke is an American fiddle and banjo tune from the Kentucky. The melody of the song is mostly stepwise. Last two bars include the notes G and A.

Old Joe Clarke

American Fiddle Song

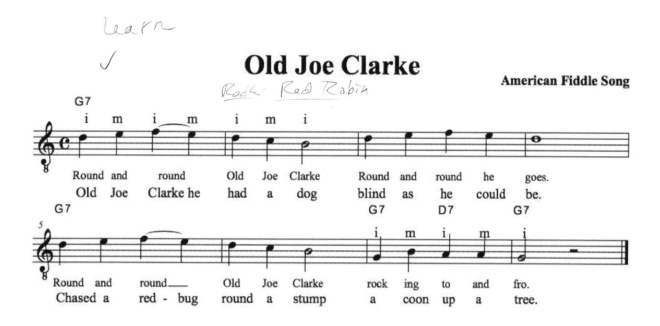

Aura Lee was a popular song among the Union and Confederate soldiers during the Civil War. The tune continued to be popular in the 20th century. In 1956 Elvis Presley adapted the melody of this song with lyrics by Ken Darby in his popular hit "Love Me Tender". Allan Sherman, comic satirist, altered the lyrics of tune with a flu-based version:

> Every time you take vaccine, take it orally [a pun on "Aura Lea"]
> As you know the other way is felt more painfully!

Practice tips

The first four-bar phrase is repeated in line two. The last four-bar erases (measure 13-16) begins similarly. If you master the first phrase you will have more than half the melody learned. The melody of the first three bars of Aura Lee has its challenges, particularly measure two. Prepare the fingers as you would a chord (see below). This is especially in measure two; prepare fourth and second fingers (for "D" and "A" respectively) like a chord (see below).

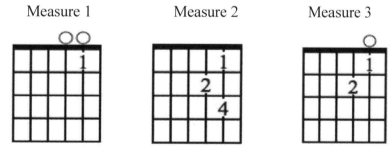

Eight of the eleven notes in line three is the note E. The other three descend and ascend on string 2 (D-C-D). Preparing the fingers - four and two - on the fingered notes in measure 11 can help lower the difficulty. In 1956, Elvis took this 95-year old melody, added new lyrics, and created one of most enduring hits. Sing along with Norah Jones beautiful cover, https://youtu.be/-gzC29VwE1A .

Week 9 Practice Calendar

Three Goals:

(1) Sight read eight notes covered on strings 1, 2, and 3 in position one.

(2) Learn new chord D7. Master chord changes C to D7, D7 to G7.

(3) Master the three strum-rhythm patterns and the arpeggio patterns (pima, pami).

	Sunday	Monday	Tuesday	Wednesday	Thursday	Friday	Saturday
Scales							
Chords							
Arpeggio							
Strum							
New Songs							
Old Songs							

Practice - minimum of 30 - 40 minutes per day

Scales: 1-2 minute per day (Mixolydian mode)
 (1) One octave at quarter note (one second) - four times.
    Play each tone twice to ensure you alternate fingering.
 (2) One octave at eighth note (half a second) - four times.
    Play each tone twice to ensure you alternate fingering.

Chord changes - 3 minute a day
 (1) Synchronized movement - fingers move and arrive at the same
    time **C- D7, D7 - G7; C - 3 minute a day**
 (2) Four times for each chord change up to minute for each until mastered.

Arpeggio Patterns: p-i-m-i, p-m-i-m, p-i-m-a; p-a-m-i (10 minutes a day)
 (1) Two patterns a day: quarter note pace - seven times
 (2) Observe and correct position, follow through
 (3) Practice at four different dynamic levels: p, mp, mf, F

Strum Patterns - (10 minutes a day)
 (1) Two patterns a day
 (2) Accurate rhythm of the strum with index finger
 (3) Strike correct number of strings
 (4) Aim for a full down strum, and light up strung

Song repertoire - (20 minutes a day)
 (1) New songs: Old Joe Clark, Aura Lee
 (2) Review: Preludio, Jambalaya, Mary Had a Little Lamb, Heart and Soul

Lesson 10: Accidentals & Scaling the Fingerboard

Lesson ten introduces accidentals - sharps, flats, and natural signs - which are used to alter the natural pitch of a note a semitone, one fret. When these symbols are used at the beginning of a piece they indicate the "key" of a piece and correspondingly the specific scale (series of tones) the piece is based on. This lesson will also include the following major scales: C, G, D, E, A.

Accidentals

A **sharp** sign (#) placed before a note indicates the pitch is raised a semitone (one fret) higher than its natural tone. On the guitar, raising a note a semitone is achieved by shortening the string length by one fret. For example, the note A played on the third string fret two; the note A sharp is on fret three. A sharp sign placed within a measure is "in effect" for one measure; it is automatically cancelled by the following bar line.

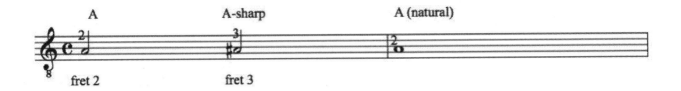

A **flat** sign (b) placed before a note indicates the pitch is lowered a semitone (one fret) higher than the natural tone. On the guitar, this result is achieved by lengthening the string length one fret. For example, the note A played on the third string fret two; the note A flat is on fret one. A flat sign placed within a measure is "in effect" for one measure; it is automatically cancelled by the bar line.

A **natural** sign placed before a note cancels effect of a sharp or flat within a measure. The result is the note played is the "natural" pitch.

Chromatic Scale

A chromatic scale moves by semitones, the distance of one fret on the guitar. A sharp (#) indicates the tone has raised a semitone. If the note G, third open, is raised a semitone it is called G sharp (see below). Sharps are used in an ascending chromatic scale (as shown below in the left diagram) indicate the direction of the scale is going up.

In contrast, the chromatic scale (in the diagram on the right) is moving down the chromatic ladder. The flat (b) sign indicates the tone has been lowered a semitone, one fret. Flats, in this case, are used indicate the direction of the scale is moving downward one fret at a time. Beginning on G, third string open, play each successive note of the scale chart. Use the third (ring) finger for notes on the third, and the fourth finger for notes on fret four. Say the name of each tone as you play it. Watch the position of the left-hand fingers. Be especially careful there is adequate separation between the first and second finger; this ensures the third and fourth finger will be able to comfortably reach the third and fourth frets respectively. Leave the fingers down as you ascend on each string. Prepare all the three or four fingers on the descent. Play the scale below four times each day.

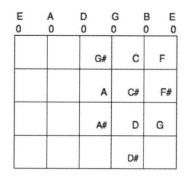 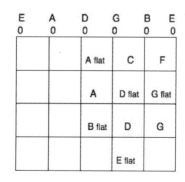

Reading the Chromatic Scale

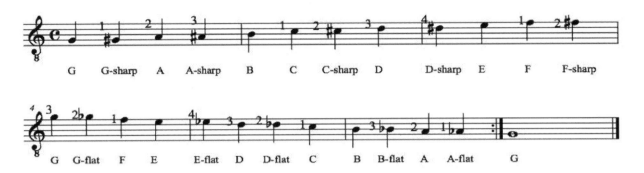

Major Scale

A **major scale** consists of a pattern of two whole steps, a half step, three whole steps and a half step. The fingering of the C major scale below begins on the note C (second string first fret) is fingered on the second string only. The position marking to the left indicates the placement of the first finger. In position one the first finger is positioned on the first fret, position five it is on fret five; position ten it is on fret ten. Play the scale form five times slowly.

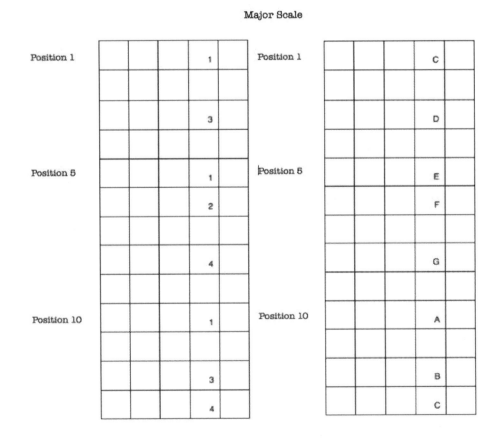

Examining the distance between the notes is easier to visualize on one string. The distance between

C and D (D and E) is two frets (two semitones); whereas the distance between E and F (B and C) is one fret (one semitone or a half step). Playing a G major scale moving across the strings contains the same pattern of intervals; the fingering, however, is different.

G Major Scale

The G major scale is composed of eight tones in the following pattern of intervals: two whole steps, a half step, three whole steps and a half step. The seventh note in a G-major scale needs to be raised a semitone (to F sharp) to be consistent to the pattern of intervals for a major-scale (see below).

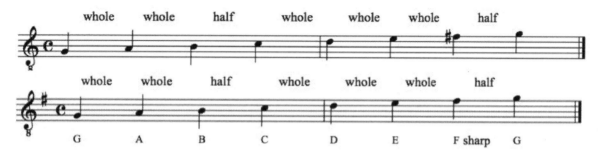

If a piece of music is built on a G-major scale it is in the key of G. At the beginning of a piece in the key of G major, a sharp is placed on the top line (f sharp) indicating the piece is in key is G major and **all f's** are sharp (unless a natural sign is used to cancel the sharp). At each subsequent five-line system a sharp on the fifth (f) line reminds the performer the key is G major and all f tones are sharp, raised a semitone.

Bach in a Minuet:

The piece below is in the key of G major as evidenced by the F sharp sign on the top line of the treble clef. The piece was inspired by Johann Sebastian Bach's minuet in G and a female Rock group. In 1965 lyrics were added to the tune and meter was changed from simple-triple meter (3/4 time) to a simple quadruple meter (4/4 time). The song was called "A Lover's Concerto." The Toys, a female rock vocal group, first recorded the song. Numerous other Like the 1960 rock version, this piece is in 4/4 time. The tempo is moderate. The first section has four stepwise (scale like) eighth note figures; the first two go up, the latter two go down. The piece is in binary form, two sections. The first section is repeated and has two endings. The first ends on the note "A"; the second ends on G.

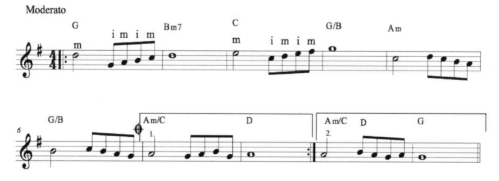

The second section of the piece is different from both Bach's original and Lover's Concerto. It is in E-minor. This melody in this section is more comprised of chord tones, melodic notes that are congruent with the chords. For example, the chord in measure 11 is an E minor (e-g-b) chord, the melody is comprised of open strings (B, E, G). In contrast melody in measure 15 - 18 and 24 - 27 moves mostly by step. The instructional video is https://youtu.be/0CHBq72doWg .

The D.C. (Da Capo) al Coda appearing at the end of the fourth system instructs the performer to return to the beginning until the coda sign (a circle with a cross) at the beginning of measure seven in Section A. The coda, line five, is the ending of the piece. Note the last four bars are in 3/4 time. Molto rit. (ritard) indicates the tempo should slow down in the last two bars. Play along at slow tempo https://youtu.be/qwkosdQKD8Y .

Practice strategy:

Read and identify the notes of the first two bars without playing the tones. Picture the fingerboard as you read the notes. Next try saying the note names, tapping your foot, and picture the fingerboard, with the correct timing. Do this twice. Having identified what notes to play, when to play them, and even what fingers you will use to play them - play the tune. The first two steps in this process should amount to a minute of your time. You will be tempted to just go for it; however, if you keep to practice strategy you will execute the notes the first time with greater accuracy and success. One popular rendition of the song was sung by Diana Ross and the Supremes. **Sing along with** https://youtu.be/BU8MuWJm_cY .

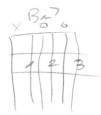

Lyrics to Lover's Concerto - Sandy Linzer and Denny Randell

How gentle is the rain, that falls softly on the meadow;
Birds high upon the trees serenade the flow'rs with their melodies.
Oh, see there beyond the hill, the bright colors of the rainbow;
Some magic from above made this day for us, just to fall in love.

Scales, Keys, and the Circle of Fifths

The only major key without a sharp or a flat is C major. Each successive sharp key which is five tones away. Starting on C the next key is G with one sharp (F#). After G major is D major with two sharps (F# and C#). After D is A major with three sharps (F#, C#, and G#), and E major with four sharps (F#, C#, G#, and D#). The major-scale form below is movable across the fingerboard of the guitar. Practice this scale form in following different positions on the guitar and you are learning to play in five keys.

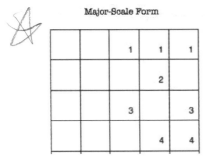

Major-Scale Form | C-Major Scale, Position 5

Scale Practice

Scale practice is an essential daily activity for skill development on any musical instrument. On the most basic level, scale practice is an excellent way to direct and correct hand position and finger placement. It is good for developing better coordination and synchronization of both hands. Scales can be used to work on dynamics and melodic shaping of a scale tones, as well as articulation, such as staccato (detached tones) and legato (connected tones). Practice playing the scale form in each of the following five successive positions two times daily. Practice with https://youtu.be/RrloFjO6a4k .

Key Position

Key	Position
C	5
G*	1
D	7
A	2
E	9

Major-Scale form

*N.B. The G-major scale form in first position has a different fingering because it uses open strings. The fingering for G-major is open G, two on A, open B, one on C, four (fret three) on D, open E, two on F-sharp, and four on G (fret three).

Scale and Chord Practice

The following practice combines the moveable major scale form and I – V7 chord progression in five keys: C, G, D, A, and E. Team up with a friend and play this exercise. After playing the scale four times try creating (improvising) a tune of your own. The following link is an excellent practice tool: https://youtu.be/RrloFjO6a4k .

The Written Notes of the Major Scale in Five Keys

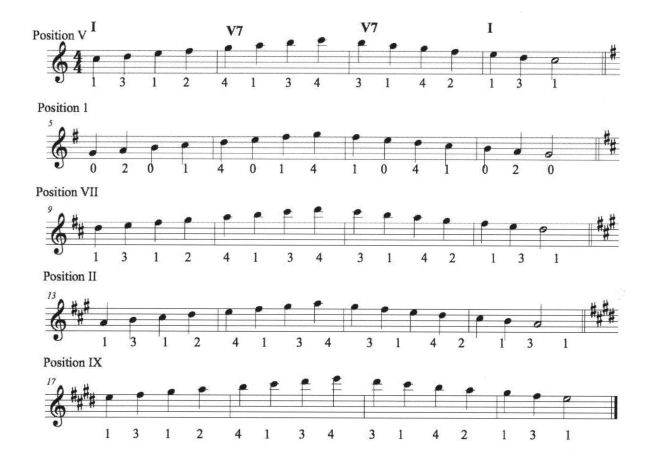

Ear-Training Challenge!

Pick out by ear the song Ode to Joy. You may choose any of the major keys. The starting note is the third note in a major scale. There is one note which is outside the box, the one octave major- scale form. Afterwards modulate the key by simply changing the position of the fingers.

The first section of chords for Ode to Joy use only two chords: I and V7. This chord progression is presented in Lesson 12 five keys listed above.

Lesson 10 Practice Calendar

Two Goals:

(1) Introduce accidentals, two new scale forms. Learn movable major scale fingering, as well as two scale forms (chromatic and major) in position 1.

(2) Learn to read music in the key of G: Bach in a Minuet.

	Sunday	Monday	Tuesday	Wednesday	Thursday	Friday	Saturday
Scales							
Chords							
Arpeggio							
Strum							
New Songs							
Old Songs							

Practice - minimum of 30 - 40 minutes per day

Scales: 2 minute per day (Major, chromatic mode)
 (1) Five one octave major scales (C, G, D, A, E) - two times each.
 (2) One octave at eighth note (half a second) - two times each.

Chord changes - 3 minute a day
 (1) Review and improve chord changes: **C- D7, D7 - G7; C - 3 minute a day**
 (2) Four times for each chord change up to minute for each until mastered.

Arpeggio Patterns: p-i-m-i, p-m-i-m, p-i-m-a; p-a-m-i (10 minutes a day)
 (1) Two patterns a day: quarter note pace - seven times
 (2) Observe and correct position, follow through
 (3) Practice at four different dynamic levels: p, mp, mf, F

Strum Patterns - (5 minutes a day)
 (1) Two patterns a day
 (2) Accurate rhythm of the strum with index finger
 (3) Strike correct number of strings
 (4) Aim for a full down strum, and light up strung

Song repertoire - (20 minutes a day)
 Bach in a Minuet – Melody in the key of G
   i. **Bach in a Minuet -** Simple chords for "A Lover's Concerto" :
 G |D |C |G | Am7 | G | Am7 | D7   :||
 Strum, arpeggiate, & sing: Jambalaya, Mary Had a Little Lamb, Aura Lee, Paperback Writer, Heart and Soul
 Optional: Pick out the melody Ode to Joy by ear using the major-scale form

Lesson 11: Jazz Vamp: Dominant-Seventh Led Circle of Fifths

This lesson introduces the chord A7 along with two related chord progressions. Both progressions use a series of circular dominant-seventh chords. The function of a dominant-seventh chords is for the produced harmonic tension to resolve to the tonic. These progressions exploit this function to lead the listener around the circle of fifths before resolving on the tonic: from A7 to D7 to G7 to C, and E7 to A7 to D7 to G7 to C. The principle these progressions can be found in the music of Bach, Vivaldi, Mozart, Haydn, and Beethoven. It also appears in a multitude of Ragtime and Jazz standards, songs such as After Your Gone and Ain't Misbehavin', Hello My Baby and Five Foot Two.

Progression 1

Progression 1 introduces the chord A7. The inclusion of the first finger on the A7 is not an accident. Continuing to hold the first finger from the previous C chord prepares the first finger for the G7 chord. Practice strumming each chord twice. The resulting two-bar "vamp" will likely sound familiar to your ears. It was used as a background progression for stand-up comics in the days of vaudeville.

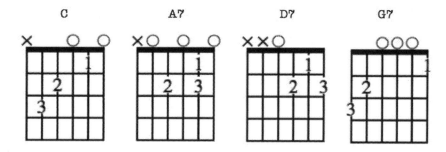

The lengthened presentations of progression one and two should be played as it would in an upbeat swinging ragtime tempo. Progression 1 is used the song Hello My Baby; the second is found in the roaring 20s Five Foot Two.

Progression 1

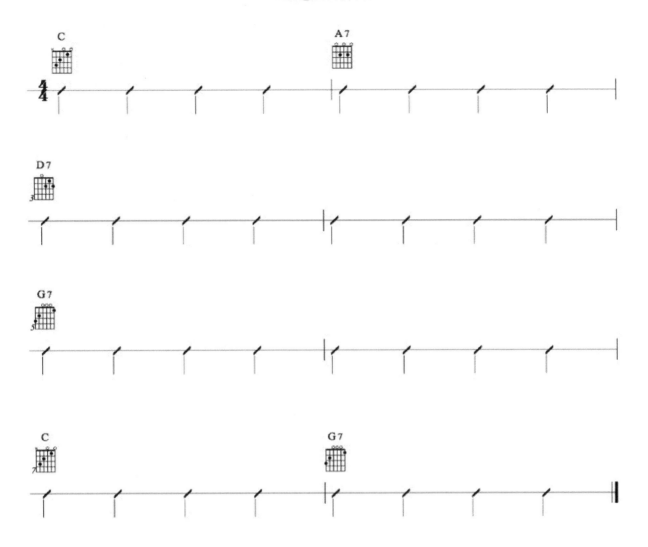

Progression 2

This progression is commonly used as a turn-around progression at the end of a section of music. Instead of resolving to a tonic chord (C major) for eight beats this progression is substituted. Practice strumming each chord twice.

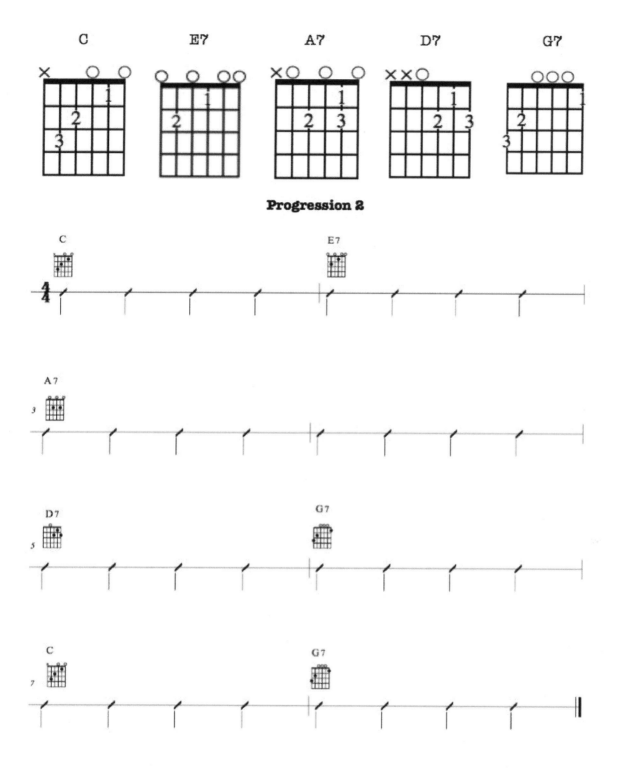

Ragged Time

The following fun and challenging piece is in a ragtime style. Its name, Ragged Time, was the first descriptive term used to describe this syncopated style of music in the late 19th century. Later the name changed to Ragtime. Ragtime employs cakewalk rhythms and chromatic melodic lines associated with ragtime and jazz.

Cakewalk Rhythm

This rhythm was common in the African songs the slaves sang on the plantation. The cakewalk dance was coined in association to a competitive dance among slaves of the plantation. The winner was declared with the line: That takes the cake! The reward for the winning pair was a sweet cake. The rhythm, as shown below, became known as a cakewalk rhythm.

D U D U D U

Section A uses the progression one in the first eight bars of the piece. Progression two is used in the B section (measures 9-16). Measure seven and eight are tacit; i.e., there is no harmonic accompaniment. If the syncopated rhythms in measures 1, 3, 5, and 7 feel tricky to navigate, practice the rhythm as a strum (see rhythm exercise below). Be sure tap your foot and feel the down and up movement of the individual beats.

Ragged Time

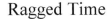

Peter Joseph Zisa

If you enjoy Ragged Time, try the next two classic Rag and early jazz hits. Sing along with Hello My Baby (for verses) https://youtu.be/a3snyPWw5kQ . You will note from this rendition this is an excellent call and response song. There are additional verses on the recording you may wish to include. Can you identify to chords to the verses?

The second song, Sing Five Foot Two, was first recorded by the California Ramblers in 1925. It was recorded by many other artists including Guy Lombardo and Kenny Gardner, https://youtu.be/5UWOiDJNAuA . The song was also a favorite of the barbershop quartets; here is such an example https://youtu.be/c1j0BgBj4SE

[handwritten: Tony Orlando & Dawn — G — Tie Yellow Ribbon — Sweet Gypsy Rose]

Hello My Baby
"Howard and Emerson"

```
C                A7             D7
Hello my baby - ---- hello my honey --- hello my ragtime gal
G7                    C            G7
Send me a kiss by wire - - honey my heart's on fire
```
[handwritten: Top strings]

```
C                A7               D7
If you refuse me -- honey you'll lose me -- then you'll be left alone

      G7              C        (G7)
Oh baby telephone and tell me I'm your own
```

Five Foot Two
Percy Weinrich music and Jack Mahoney lyrics

```
C             E7         A7
Five foot two - Eyes of blue - Oh what those five foot can do!

D7      G7    C      (G7)
Has anybody seen my gal?

C              E7              A7
Turned up nose - turned down hose - she never had another pose

D7      G7    C
Has anybody seen my gal?

E7                                       A7
Now if you run into - -  a five foot two   covered with fur

D7                        G7
Diamond rings and all them things - - bet your life it ain't her

C              E7            A7
But could she love - could she woo - could she could she could she coo

D7     G7    C       (G7)       C
Has anybody seen my gal?
```

85

Lesson 11 Practice Calendar

Goals:

(1) Master two Jazz Vamp chord progressions: C - A7 - D7 - G7 and C - E7 - A7 - D7 - G7

(2) Master the melody & chords of Ragged Time.

(3) Sing and play Hello My Baby and Five Foot Two.

	Sunday	Monday	Tuesday	Wednesday	Thursday	Friday	Saturday
Scales							
Chords							
Arpeggio							
Strum							
New Songs							
Old Songs							

Practice - minimum of 30 - 40 minutes per day.

Scales: 2 minutes per day

    (1) One octave at quarter note (one second) - four times.

    (2) One octave at eighth note (half a second) - four times.

    (3) Chromatic scale at quarter note (one second) - twice

Chord changes - 3 minutes per day

    (1) Synchronized movement - fingers move and arrive at the same time.

    (2) Legato

    (3) Coordinated with strum or arpeggio

Arpeggio Patterns: 10 minutes per day

    (1) Two patterns a day: quarter note pace - seven times

    (2) Observe and correct position, follow through

    (3) Practice at four different dynamic levels: p, mp, mf, F

Strum Patterns - 10 minutes

    (1) Two patterns a day

    (2) Accurate rhythm of the strum with index finger

    (3) Strike correct number of strings

    (4) Aim for a full down strum, and light up strung

Song repertoire - 15 minutes

    (1) New Songs: Hello My Baby, Five Foot Two, and Ragged Time
    (2) Review Lover's Concerto, Heart and Soul.

Lesson 12: Chord Summary & Harmonic Progressions & Transpositions

So far you have learned the following chords: C, Cmaj7, Em, E, E7, G, G7, Am, Am7, A7, Dm, D, and D7. This lesson we will review the chords above and add the following new chords: A, Bm7, B7, and F#m7. Additionally, you will learn how to play four-chord progressions in five keys.

I – V7; V7 – I Progression

This progression is the most foundational progression. As we learned earlier, this progression is found in traditional folk and popular music. You first learned this progression in the Key of C; the two chords were C and G7. If the melody of the song was not in your vocal range you could change the chords to a key that accommodated your vocal range. If it was too low for instance you could raise the key a step, from C to D. The two chords would then be D and A7; D being the tonic chord and A7 the dominant-seventh chord (five tones above D).

||: I | V7 |V7 |I   :||

What if you wished to change to the key of G? G would be the tonic (I) chord. What chord would be the dominant-seventh chord? Count five notes up to arrive at the answer: G (a, b, c) and ?! Got it? The two chord I – V7 progression in G is G and D7. Play this game a little longer. Name the two chords for the key of D and A.

Key	I Tonic Chord	V7 Dominant-Seventh Chord
C	C	G7
G	G	D7
D	D	A7
A	A	E7
E	E	B7

Transposition

Singing and accompanying yourself on the guitar sometimes runs into difficulty when the range of sung notes of the song do not match your vocal range. What to do? The solution may be change the key. If the song feels too high try a lowering the key.

I - V7 Progression

The chord progression below is shown in four keys. Take a song you have learned, such as Go Tell Aunt Rhody. You learned in C major; change the key to D major. Then try playing and singing it in A major. Which one sounded higher? Which one was easier to sing?

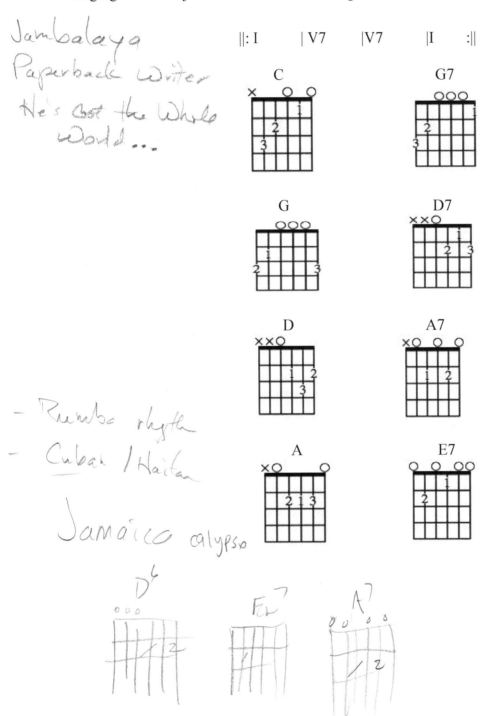

I-ii-V7-I Progression

I-ii-V7-I progression has been popular chord progression for about 300 years. It may be found in the music of Mozart and popular music in the 20th and 21st century. One example is Harry Belafonte's hit Jamaica Farewell. Try singing and playing this song, or another with the same chord progression, in different keys.

I - ii - V7 - I Progression

||: I | ii |V7 |I :||

C	Dm	G7
G	Am7	D7
D	Em7	A7
A	Bm7	E7

I-vi-ii-V7-I Progression

Equally popular with the last two progressions, is the I-vi-ii-V7-I progression. It appeared in the song Heart and Soul in the key of C. Many of the love songs of the 1950s, such as Blue Moon, use this progression. Try singing and playing this song, or another with the same chord progression, in different keys. With the exception of the key of A, these chords may be strummed or arpeggiated fingerstyle. The F#m7 in the key of A is best arpeggiated.

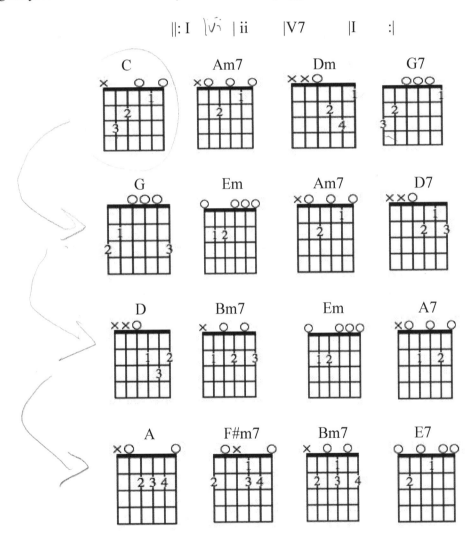

The Capo and Harmonic Transposition

A **capo** is a device that changes the "head of the fingerboard". It is an easy way to change the key without changing the chord shapes. As you recall moving up the fingerboard one fret is the distance of a semitone or half step. If you position the capo on the second fret of the guitar it will raise the pitch of the instrument a whole step higher. The C chord form below has been raised a whole step. The result is the fingering shape below is now a D chord! If a song is too low to comfortable sing using is an easy way to transpose.

There are many variety of capos at the local guitar shop. I would recommend one which is easy to put on and not so large and cumbersome, like the one above. The capo below, for example, is solidly constructed with an nonabrasive rubber material on the strings, fingerboard, and back of the neck.

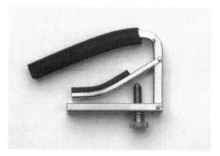

Transposition Using Four Major Chord Shapes

The charts below show how the position of the capo changes the chord name and the corresponding key of the major-chord shapes.

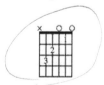

Fret Position	Chord Key
2	D
4	E
5	F
7	G

Fret Position	Chord Key
2	A
4	B
5	C
7	D

Fret Position	Chord Key
2	E
3	F
5	G
7	A

Fret Position	Chord Key
2	B
3	C
5	D
7	E

Lesson 12 Practice Calendar

Goals:

(1) Learn three new chords A, Bm7, and F#m7.

(2) Learn to sing and play songs using three progressions in four keys.

	Sunday	Monday	Tuesday	Wednesday	Thursday	Friday	Saturday
Scales							
Chords							
Arpeggio							
Strum							
New Songs							
Old Songs							

Practice - minimum of 30 - 40 minutes per day.

Scales: 2 minutes per day

    (1) One octave at quarter note (one second) - four times.

    (2) One octave at eighth note (half a second) - four times.

    (3) Chromatic scale at quarter note (one second) - twice

Chord changes - 3 minutes per day

    (1) Synchronized movement - fingers move and arrive at the same time.

    (2) Legato

    (3) Coordinated with strum or arpeggio

Arpeggio Patterns: 10 minutes per day

    (1) Two patterns a day: quarter note pace - seven times

    (2) Observe and correct position, follow through

    (3) Practice at four different dynamic levels: p, mp, mf, F

Strum Patterns - 10 minutes

    (1) Two patterns a day

    (2) Accurate rhythm of the strum with index finger

    (3) Strike correct number of strings

    (4) Aim for a full down strum, and light up strung

Song repertoire - 15 minutes

    (1) New Songs: Jamaica Farewell…

    (2) Review Lover's Concerto, Heart and Soul, Aunt Rhody, Jamabaya

Lesson 13: Open Bass Strings and Varied Arpeggios

This lesson introduces three open bass strings: D, A, and E. These bass notes will be played by the thumb. Notes on the third, second, and first string will be played with the index (i), middle (m), and ring finger (a). You will read music that includes these open strings as part of a variety of arpeggiated patterns using the chords A, D, and E7. The chord progression in Etude 1 and 2 is used in numerous popular songs, such as Bob Dylan's Blowing in the Wind. After you are skilled playing the chord progression and arpeggio patterns, try singing the song "Blowing in the Wind."

Open Bass Strings

The three open bass notes - D, A, and E - are tuned in fourths. In the key of A, these bass notes could represent the tonic (I), sub-dominant (IV) and dominant (V) chords: A, D, and E respectively. The arpeggio below represents one way these chords may be played. Upon further examination of the chords, you might notice the fingering of the chords includes only the chord tones played. Strumming an E chord, for example, includes two more fingers in first position and involves striking all six strings. The E chord below, in contrast, has four tones on four strings: six, three, two, and one.

Finger the chord below and play the arpeggiated pattern twice for each measure. Use rest stroke on the bass notes for the A chord and E chord. Initially count two beats for each tone. Increase the rate of the arpeggio to quarter-note and eighth-note pace as your skill improves and level confidence increases.

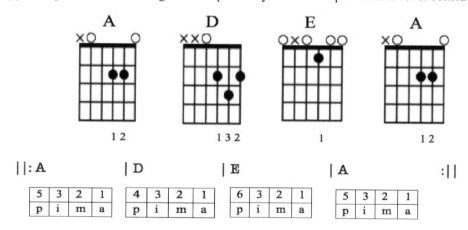

Notation of Open Bass Strings

The bass notes on the guitar extend below the staff; ledger lines are added to represent these tones. Use rest stroke with the thumb to strike the bass notes. Keep the top knuckles of the right hand over the three treble strings.

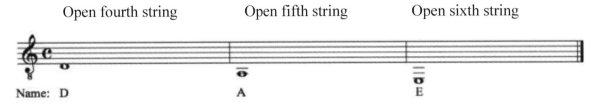

The chords in the song below are the same (tonic, sub-dominant, and dominant) chords as the exercise above. In the first eight bars the arpeggiated pattern is in reversed order: P-a-m-i-a-m-i-a. The bass note is this section is a tonic-pedal tone ("A"). This use of tonic pedal elicits a stated tension to the changing harmony. The bass notes in the last eight bars vary from measure to measure. How would you describe this change in the accompaniment figure and added bass notes in the section of the piece.

The following four bars is the written notation of the previous arpeggiated pattern of the chords A, D, E, and A. The accidentals are necessary to make each of these chords major; without the raised notes in each measure, the chords would be minor.

The accidentals, sharps or flats, written at the beginning of the system is key signature. The key signature indicates the key and the accidentals associated with the key. The key of A major has three sharps F#, C#, and G#. Note below the same four chords as those above with the key signature (F#, C#, and G#) to the left of the time signature.

Practice slowly playing the arpeggiated chords above. To better mentally prepare and assess your progress begin by allowing two beats between every struck note. After four repetitions of the first line play the line in strict time, allowing one beat for each note.

Prep for Etudes 1 & 2

The following etudes are primarily use the tonic (A), sub-dominant (D), and dominant (E) chords in the key of A. The lone exception is the F#m7 (sub-mediant) chord. The fingering of the previous A chord should be fingered with the second and third fingers on A and C# respectively to best prepare the fingers.

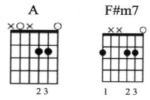

Etude 1 Chord Progression

The following 16 chord forms represents the harmonic progression of Etude 1. The bass note in the first eight bars is a drone (repeated tone) on the note A. The bass notes of line three and four change with the chord. Using a simple p-i-m-a pattern would be helpful while getting comfortable with the progression.

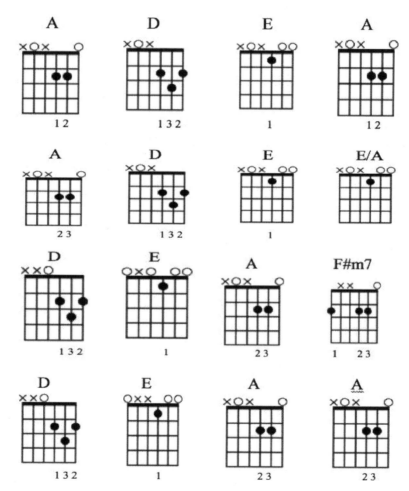

Etude 1

The arpeggiated pattern of Etude 1 is P-a-m-i-a-m-i-a. The bass note is this section is the tonic-pedal tone (A). This use of tonic pedal elicits static tension against the changing harmony. The bass notes in the last eight bars vary from measure to measure. How would you describe this change in the accompaniment figure and added bass notes in the section of the piece?

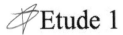

Peter Joseph Zisa

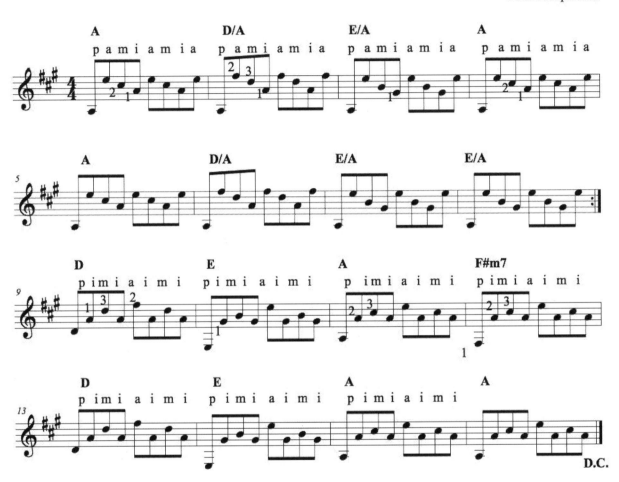

Re-voiced Chord Forms

Etude 2 employs the same chord progression and Etude 1. The upper voicing of the chords during the last eight bars in Etude 2, however, extends to fifth position (see below). The chord shape of the first two chords is the same; the second chord, "E", is in position four and the bass note is a low "E". Moving the hand up and down the fretboard may present challenges. Begin by practicing shifting the position of the first two chords. Be careful to maintain the chord shape while you move the hand up two frets.

The third chord in the sequence moves to an "A" chord in fifth position; note how the first and third finger switch strings. It may be helpful to practice the fingering change in position four (four times) before attempting to make the fingering change while moving from fourth position to fifth position.

The last chord is an "A" chord in position one. It may be helpful to practice the parallel movement of the first and second fingers to the third and second string. Maintaining concentration on the parallel movement of the fingers while moving the hand down to position one is best down slowly. It can also be helpful to mentally visualize this movement four times before attempting to execute it.

As you work to master this left-hand chord forms in higher positions on the guitar consider using the simple p-i-m-a arpeggio pattern. Play the new fingering four times. When you feel comfortable with executing both hands turn to reading the notes in Etude 2.

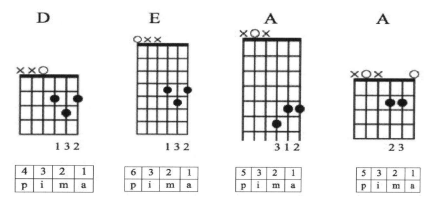

Arpeggiated Variation

The arpeggiated patterns are varied in Etude 2. The first section still employs an "A" drone. The rhythmic grouping of the arpeggio pattern is asymmetrical: p-i-m-p-i-m-p-m. The syncopated pattern follows a **1**-2-3-**1**-2-3-**1**-2. This rhythmic pattern is frequently found in South American dance forms like the rumba.

The arpeggiated pattern of the second section is more legato and melodically driven. The chord progression of Etude 2 is the same as Dylan's *Blowing in the Wind*. The highest voice on string one of the pattern could be a counter melody to the sung melody.

Compare and contrast the emotional impact of the first eight bars of the two Etudes. Etude 2 employs the same chord progression (series of chords) as Etude 1. How is the arpeggiated accompaniment of the first section (eight bars) different from Etude 1? How are they the similar?

The choice of arpeggiated pattern is an important consideration. A four-note pattern of quarter notes will have different energy from an eighth note pattern. Similarly, a pattern with only one bass note per bar with sound slower (conveying less rhythmic energy) than a pattern with two or more bass notes per bar. With simple varied chord forms in the upper register of the guitar a counter melody may be created.

Etude 2

Peter Joseph Zisa

Transposition Assignment

Transpose the chord progression above to the key of C, G, and D.

Lesson 13 Practice Calendar

Two Goals:

(1) Learn to read and play the open bass notes with the thumb along with the four arpeggiated accompaniment patterns.

(2) Develop smooth I-IV-V chord changes with various chord voicing in the key of A.

	Sunday	Monday	Tuesday	Wednesday	Thursday	Friday	Saturday
Scales							
Chords							
Arpeggio							
Strum							
New Songs							
Old Songs							

30-40 minutes per day

Scales: 3 minutes per day
- (1) One octave at quarter note (one second) - four times. Play each tone twice to ensure you alternate fingering.
- (2) One octave at eighth note (half a second) - four times. Play each tone twice to ensure you alternate fingering.

Chord changes - As applicable (3 minutes per day)
- (1) Synchronized movement - fingers move and arrive at the same time.
- (2) Legato
- (3) Coordinated with picking

Four New Arpeggio Patterns: (3 minutes per day; 45 seconds each)
- (1) Two patterns a day: quarter note pace - four time minimum
- (2) Observe and correct position, follow through
- (3) Practice at four different dynamic levels: p, mp, mf, F

Strum Patterns - (3 minutes per day)
- (1) Two patterns a day
- (2) Accurate rhythm of the strum with index finger
- (3) Strike correct number of strings
- (4) Aim for a full down strum, and light up strung

Song repertoire -
- **NEW:** Etude 1 and 2 (5 minutes each) Blowin' in the Wind
- **REVIEW** selections from established repertoire.**(3 minutes)**
- **Transposition Assignment:** Transpose Etude (Blowin' in the Wind) to C, G, and D.

Lesson 14: Juggling: Combining Melody and Bass

Lesson 14 introduces a new technical and musical challenge: learning a piece that has both melody and bass notes. The use of the open bass strings of the guitar represent the supporting harmony. The melody is a simple easy to memorize tune composed of short repeated melodic units. After you learn the melody, you will then add the open string bass notes to suggest harmonic texture.

The Tune: A Simple Melodic Motif

The melodic figure in measures one and two consists of a six-note motif. The first four notes on string three and the last two notes a minor third figure. The second time this figure occurs in the line the last two notes (minor third) is omitted. Placing the thumb (p) gently on the fourth string is recommended. Play the six notes slowly (allowing two beats for each note) four times. Then play the first line.

Repeat this same learning strategy with the melody on the second line.

Repeat this same learning strategy. The added difficulty in this line is the use of the "a" finger. It may be helpful to practice the right hand alone with the thumb (p) positioned on string 5.

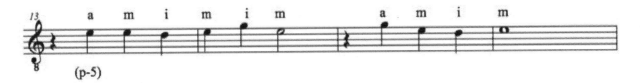

Adding the Bass

The bass notes of Rockin' the Boat are the open bass strings. Strike the first bass note using rest stroke with the thumb. Continuing to rest the thumb on the adjacent string, play the following six-note melodic motif. The bass note should continue to ring while you are playing the melody. On beat four of the next measure, the thumb strikes the bass note again.

The third and fourth measure of the line begins the same way as the first two measures. The fourth measure contains the last note of the melodic phrase. Beginning on the second beat of this measure, three repeated bass notes occur. Follow the same procedure in learning the following two lines (lines two and four of the piece).

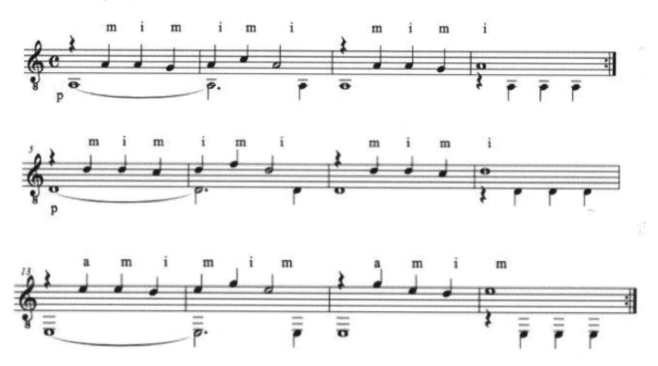

The Coda

The coda is the ending of the piece. The ending phrase may be divided into two parts. Part 1 is the first seven melodic notes of the ending phrase. Part 2 is composed nearly entirely of eighth notes contains nine melodic notes.

Practice Strategy:

The coda (ending) is last line of the piece. It is a kind of rock cadenza (rock solo). The melodic structure is more chromatic (has more accidentals) and technically challenging. Breaking the melody into smaller melodic units is a helpful learning strategy to make the process easier.

Begin by practice playing motifs #1 and #2 four times slowly allowing one full beat for each note before playing at a faster tempo. Estimated practice time on this is about one minute; after which, you may try practicing each unit at tempo. Follow the same procedure for motif #3. Then slow play #3 slowly. Allow two days of slow practice before trying to connect the motifs at tempo.

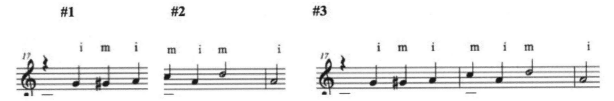

On the third and fourth day combining them into six and eight note motifs.

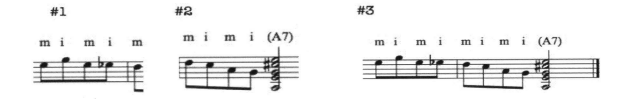

On the fifth day, play the entire four-bar ending at half tempo, allowing one beat for eighth notes and two beats for quarter notes. Repeat this four times. Then play the entire line a couple of times at tempo.

Lesson 14 Practice Calendar

Two Goals:

(1) Learn to read and play a piece with both a melody and bass part.

(2) Improve skill of using rest stroke with the thumb and free stroke with i, m, a.

	Sunday	Monday	Tuesday	Wednesday	Thursday	Friday	Saturday
Scales							
Chords							
Arpeggio							
Strum							
New Songs							
Old Songs							

30 – 45 minutes a day

Scales: 2 minutes per day (Major scale)
    (1) One octave at quarter note (one second) - four times.
        Major scale in the Key of C, G, D, A, E
    (2) Shape melodic contour of scale. Begin **mp** and crescendo up to **F,** on the descent decrescendo to **mp.**
    (3) Move right hand placement and experiment with tone color.
    (4) Experiment with staccato (detached) effect. Strike string with one digit (e.g. "i") and immediately stop the resonating string with another (e.g. "m").

Chord changes - As applicable (3 minutes per day)
    (1) Improve smoothness of difficult chord changes. Synchronized movement - fingers move and arrive at the same time.

Four Arpeggio Patterns: (10 minutes per day)
    (1) Two patterns a day: quarter note pace - four time minimum
    (2) Observe and correct position, follow through
    (3) Practice at four different dynamic levels: p, mp, mf, F

Strum Patterns - (10 minutes per day)
    (1) Two patterns a day
    (2) Accurate rhythm of the strum with index finger
    (3) Strike correct number of strings
    (4) Aim for a full down strum, and light up strung

Song repertoire -
    New Piece: Rockin the Boat (5 minutes)
    REVIEW Strum. arpeggiate, and sing song repertoire.(15 minutes)

Lesson 15: Introduction to Spanish Flamenco & the Notes on String Four

When one thinks of the historic beginnings of the guitar, images of strumming flamenco guitar in consort with flamenco dancers and singers comes to mind. The music you will play this lesson, as you learn the fingered bass notes on the fourth string, will be in the Spanish flamenco style.

The Origins of Flamenco

The origin of flamenco is equivocal. Filipe Pedrell is considered the father of Spanish musicology. He asserted *cante flamenco* was brought to Spain by the Flemish (Flamencos) gypsy (gitano) immigrants. According to Rafiel Salillas the term *flamenco* first described the loud and boisterous Flemish military soldiers; later, the Spanish used the term to describe the spirited, wild, and virtuosic music of the (Flemish) Gypsies. Spanish artists, like Julio Romero de Torres, depicted the gitano (gypsy) culture as dark and forbidding. Gitano women were dark in appearance; the lascivious and seductive nature flamenco female dancers mercerized their audience.

Musicology scholars contend the *Spanish gitano* were originally a nomadic population from North India. This view is supported by the similarities found in the singing styles of rāgas and dance to canto flamenco style. Some of these Indian nomads traveled to Persia, others to Romania, Russia, and Flanders. The Spaniards, believing the Persian nomads were from Egypt, mistakenly referred to them as Gypsies. The strong Arab influences on the development of flamenco is evident in the similarities in performing practices, the use modal melodic formulas, and vocal ornamentation.

Francisco D'Souza

Flamenco music may be divided into three forms: cante andaluz, cante gitano or cañi (Gypsy song') and cante hondo ('deep song'). While research indicates the gitano (gypsy) population significantly contributed to the development of flamenco, they were not its sole creators.

Flamenco Strumming

One of the striking characteristics of flamenco guitar music is rhythmic strumming. Finger an E chord as shown in the guitar chart below. Placing the thumb on the fifth string strum down and up with the index finger. After two measures (six beats) of strumming move the chord form up one fret to F and continue the same strum pattern. Plant "P" on string 5 when strum down and up with the index finger.

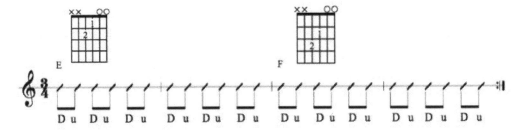

Rasqueado Strum

A rasqueado strum is a rapid rhythmic finger strumming technique. Curling your fingers over the strings, individually strike the four strings of the E or F chord; begin with the pinky (fifth finger), individually following is the ring (a) finger, the middle (m) finger, and the index (i) finger. Ideally each finger should strike all the chord tones in close succession. This auditory result is four distinct strums. When you add this technique to your strumming skills, use a full rasqueado strum on the first beat of the measures above.

Notes on the Fourth String

The notes on the fourth string are D, E, and F. The fingered notes E and F are played with the second and third finger respectively. Placing the index and middle finger on the top two strings with the top-knuckles of the hand over string two or one, play the bass notes below with the thumb (p).

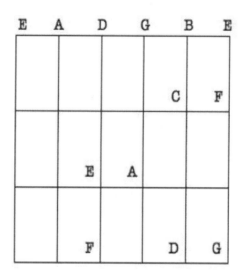

Notes on the Fourth String

Name: D   E   F
Fret: Open   2   3

Phrygian Prelude

When the moors conquered and occupied the Spanish peninsula the instruments and scale forms they used influenced the melodic language of Spain. Melodies during the middle ages music was based on the church modes: Dorian, Phrygian, Lydian, and Mixolydian. The mode most favored by composers and musicians in Spain was the phrygian mode. The first two notes of minor sounding mode are a half step away. The prelude below is in the phrygian mode. The playing style used in this piece is azapua. Azapua is a flamenco technique which forcefully accents the melodic line using only the thumb.

Begin by setting a slow tempo. The repeated use of the thumb is a deceptively difficult technique to master. When striking the string forcefully try move only the thumb when following through. Be carefully not to place your fingers on the face of the guitar.

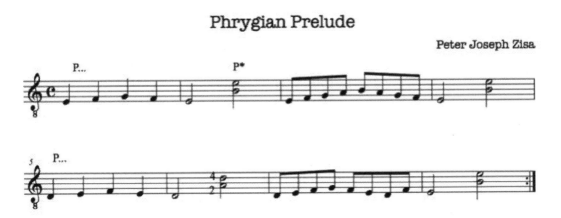

Arpeggiated Flamenco Pattern

The following pattern uses the same chord fingers as earlier flamenco strum exercise. In this case you are using the azapua technique to emphasize the arpeggiated bass melody. In the second system an open first string drone is played between the bass notes. The accompaniment style is reminiscent of famous Spanish works such as Malagueña. See practice https://youtu.be/KGe7-zMcu40 .

Piazza Di Spagna

The next piece is named after the town square Piazza Di Spagna in Rome, Italy (see picture below). It was so named because it was connected to Bourbon Spanish embassy (1721).

Piazza Di Spagna

Piazza Di Spagna is a duet. The second guitar part is an arpeggiated accompaniment of the melody. The first twelve bars of the accompaniment uses the same two chords and arpeggio pattern as the previous exercise. In measures 13-14 and 17-18 the pattern is interrupted with a D minor chord. The first guitar part makes its entry in measure 5. Guitar one plays the cante (singing) flamenco melody. It should be played with thumb (p) only. In measure 13-14 and 17-18, the player may choose to play the melody with the fingers.

Piazza di Spagna

Peter Joseph Zisa

Lesson 15 Practice Calendar

Two Goals:

(5) Learn to read and play the fingered notes on the fourth string

(2) Learn flamenco rasqueado strum and azapua technique.

	Sunday	Monday	Tuesday	Wednesday	Thursday	Friday	Saturday
Scales							
Chords							
Arpeggio							
Strum							
New Songs							
Old Songs							

30 – 45 minutes a day

Scales: 2 minutes per day (Major scale)
(1) One octave at quarter note (one second) - four times.
   Major scale in the Key of C, G, D, A, E
(2) Shape melodic contour of scale. Begin **mp** and crescendo up to **F,** on the descent decrescendo to **mp.**
(3) Move right hand placement and experiment with tone color.
(4) Experiment with staccato (detached) effect. Strike string with one digit (e.g."i") and immediately stop the resonating string with another (e.g. "m").

Chord changes - As applicable (3 minutes per day)
(1) Improve smoothness of difficult chord changes. Synchronized movement - fingers move and arrive at the same time.

Four Arpeggio Patterns: (10 minutes per day)
(1) Two patterns a day: quarter note pace - four time minimum
(2) Observe and correct position, follow through
(3) Practice at four different dynamic levels: p, mp, mf, F

Strum Patterns - (10 minutes per day)
(1) Two patterns a day
(2) Accurate rhythm of the strum with index finger
(3) Strike correct number of strings
(4) Aim for a full down strum, and light up strung

Song repertoire - (20 minutes)
New Piece: Phrygian Prelude and Piazza di Spagna (10 minutes)
REVIEW: Rockin' the Boat, (10 minutes), various repertoire songs

Lesson 16: Harps-Like Arpeggio Patterns in Triple Meter

When should you strum or arpeggiate your song accompaniment? What strum or arpeggiated pattern should you choose? Why? This lesson we consider these questions as we learn to recognize a group of related notes as arpeggiated chord tones. Along with open A note, you will add two-fingered notes (B and C) on the fifth string to your note-reading vocabulary. Adding these tones to a new arpeggiated pattern, you will learn how to recognize and play arpeggiated chord forms.

Block-chord forms versus Arpeggiated chord-form

Chord forms may be strummed (played as blocks of sounds) or arpeggiated (plucked individually) chord tones. Compare the chord forms below:

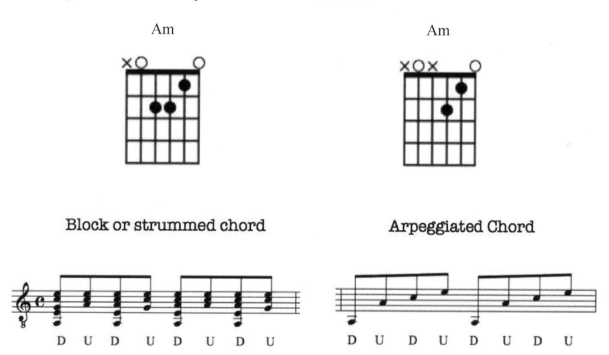

Both chords are Am chords; each contains three chord tones: A-C-E. Notice the top three tones of the block chord are identical to the arpeggiated form. The lowest tone (A), fifth string open, occurs on every down beat in form one; in contrast, the low A only twice, on beats one and three, in the arpeggiated form. How will this impact the listeners' perception of rhythm and tempo? If the arpeggiated form were written as sixteenth notes a low bass note would, like the block chord eighth-note strum, occur on every beat. How would that impact the listeners' perception of rhythm and tempo?

Rhythmic choices affect the listeners' perception of tempo. One accented bass note per bar will "feel" slower than an arpeggio or strum with four accented bass notes. When the tempo feels slower the listener feels more relaxed; conversely, a tempo that feels faster generates active and excited emotions. The choice of strum or arpeggiated patterns is an important consideration for the music therapist and music educator.

Notes on String Five

Using rest stroke with the thumb play the two-bar melody containing the notes on the fifth string. You may gently place index and middle fingers on string three and two respectively to stabilize the right hand. Check to see if the top-knuckles are forward over the treble strings and the wrist is straight.

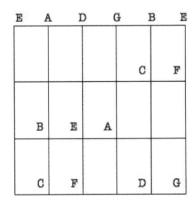

Notes on the Fifth String

The following famous melody represents from Grieg's *In the Hall of the Mountain King*. This melodic excerpt represents part of a dream-like fantasy of Peer Gynt's entry into the troll Mountain King's Hall. The piece is played loudly at a slow tempo. With each repetition, the theme accelerates and gets more excited. The entire melody may be played with the thumb. You may gently place index and middle fingers on string two and one respectively to stabilize the right hand. The range of strings played range from the fifth to the third string.

Grieg's Dream

Edvard Grieg

Arpeggio Pattern in Triple Meter

The following arpeggio pattern contains six eighth notes per bar. The thumb is responsible for the bass notes on strings six, five, and four. With the exception of the fourth string, it is recommended to use rest stroke on strings five and six. The index (i), middle (m), and ring finger (a) should strike strings three, two, and one respectively. The fingers should use free stroke to allow the chord tones to overlap and create a sonorous texture.

Notice only two fingers are needed to finger the Am chord. If the third finger is positioned over string five, the change to C will be minimally difficult. Practicing parallel movement of the second and third fingers will help improve the chord changes from C to D and from D to F major-seventh (F Maj7).

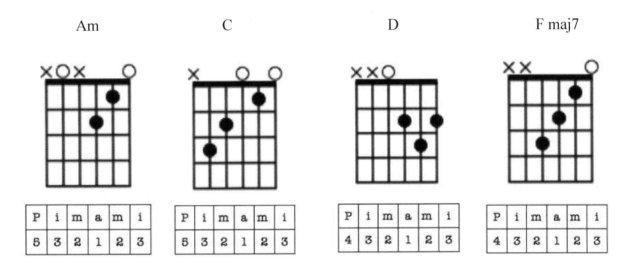

The second pattern of chords below begin the same as the first. The third chord is an E chord with a "suspended fourth". The last chord is an E chord. Because the voicing of the E and E sus4 chord does not include the fourth and fifth string no finger is required. Practice playing the pattern slowly. It may be helpful to play the pattern twice for each chord. As you gain command of the arpeggio pattern experiment executing a crescendo (gradual getting louder) and decrescendo (gradual getting softer). How does the change of dynamics affect the feeling of the progression?

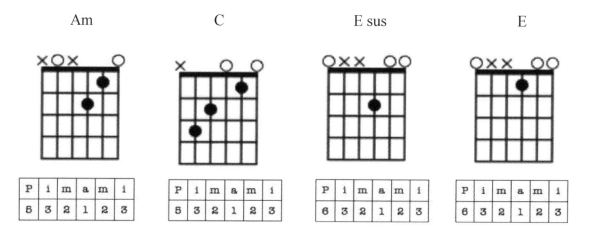

Traditional English Tune

The composer of the original English Tune is unknown. This traditional English melody later became used for the folk ballad the House of the Rising Sun. In 1964 the British rock group the Animals (https://youtu.be/hRXb7K7k7bQ) recorded arrangement of the song. The song became an instant number one success in the UK, US, and France. It has been called the first folk- rock songs, before Dylan went electric! The melody includes the new notes on string five. The arpeggiated harmonic accompaniment is an even rhythmic version the Animals distinctive arrangement. The chord progression is identical to the previous two arpeggiated chord progression. If the progression was strummed additional chord tones would have to be fingered. This arpeggiated accompaniment is more selective in its representation of the chord than the chord forms used for strumming. The E suspended and E chords, for example, only require one fingered note!

The Birth of Folk-Rock and the House of the Rising Sun

Most covers of the House of the Rising Sun adopt the same arpeggiated accompaniment the Animals' used. According to Eric Burdon, lead singer of the Animals, he first heard folk singer Johnny Handle sing the song in a club in Newcastle England. After creating their own version of the song, they began using closing song set list while on tour with Chuck Berry. Because audiences responded strongly to the song, the group interrupted their tour and recorded the song in a small studio in London.

The rhythmic figure of the Animals' arpeggio accompaniment is subtly different from the even-eighth notes in the arrangement above. After you have mastered the even eighth-note arpeggio accompaniment, you may want to modify the rhythm the arpeggio as shown below.

The Animals' Rhythmic Variation of the Arpeggiated Accompaniment:

Having learned the history of how this folk-rock song was "discovered", how different do you suppose Johnny Handle's folk "original" version might have been from the Animals' arrangement. In the absence of a recording of Handle's rendition, compare the Animals' arrangement this song (see https://youtu.be/hRXb7K7k7bQ) to the legendary Doc Watson's recording (see https://youtu.be/YeiXnyvo0d4) the House of the Rising Sun. What meter is it in? How does the difference in Doc Watson's accompaniment style alter the feeling of the song? Experiment transposing the song using a capo.

Lyrics to House of the Rising Sun – Unknown

There's a house in New Orleans, they call the rising sun.
It's been a ruin for many a poor boy, and Lord I know – I'm one.

My mother was a tailor, she sewed my new blue jeans.
My father was a gamblin' man, way down in New Orleans.

Now the only thing a gamblin' man needs, is his suitcase and trunk.
And the only time he'll be satisfied, is when he's drunk.

Mother tell all your children, not to do what I have done.
Spend your lives in sin and misery, in the house of the rising sun.

Lesson 16 Practice Calendar

Two Goals:

(1) Learn to read and play the fingered notes on the fifth string

(2) Learn triple meter arpeggio

	Sunday	Monday	Tuesday	Wednesday	Thursday	Friday	Saturday
Scales							
Chords							
Arpeggio							
Strum							
New Songs							
Old Songs							

30 – 45 minutes

Scales: 2 minutes per day (Major scale)
 (1) One octave at quarter note (one second) - four times. Major scale in the Key of C, G, D, A, E
 (2) Shape melodic contour of scale. Begin **mp** and crescendo up to **F,** on the descent decrescendo to **mp.**
 (3) Move right hand placement and experiment with tone color.
 (4) Experiment with staccato (detached) effect. Strike string with one digit (e.g."i") and immediately stop the resonating string with another (e.g."m")

Chord changes - As applicable (3 minutes per day)
 Improve smoothness of difficult chord changes. Synchronized movement - fingers move and arrive at the same time.

Four Arpeggio Patterns: (10 minutes per day)
 Two patterns a day: quarter note pace - four time minimum
 Observe and correct position, follow through
 Practice at four different dynamic levels: p, mp, mf, F

Strum Patterns - (10 minutes per day)
 (1) Two patterns a day
 (2) Accurate rhythm of the strum with index finger
 (3) Strike correct number of strings
 (4) Aim for a full down strum, and light up strung

Song repertoire - (20 minutes)
 (1) **New Piece:** Traditional English Song (House of the Rising Sun), Grieg's Dream
 (2) **REVIEW Repertoire:** Blowin' in the Wind,

Lesson 17: Smokestack Lightening!

Students often find it more difficult to learn to read and play the notes on the bass strings. This is chiefly because the bass notes on strings five and six use ledger (added staff) lines. This lesson is focused on tested strategic approaches to make this process easier and more enjoyable. First is climbing up and down the ladder, saying and playing the notes stepwise. Second is hop and skip, saying and playing thirds beginning on different notes. I recommend doing steps one and two four times a day. By the third day you should feel rather confident about the placement of the notes and their letter names. It is at this point we will turn to reading the notes on the staff. The first tuneful studies will mirror steps one and two. Because you will be familiar with the finger and letter-name pattern this process will feel easier to absorb and learn. The last two steps are two special songs in a folk and rock style.

The Notes on the Bass Strings

Below is a chart of the notes on the bass strings. Looking at the chart take note of the pattern. String six pattern is Open, Finger 1 and Finger 3 on E, F, and G respectively. Play and say the note names aloud four times. The fifth string pattern is Open, Finger 2 and Finger 3 on A, B, and C respectively. Play and say the note names aloud four times. Last, string four has the same finger pattern as string 5. String four's pattern is Open, Finger 2 and Finger 3 on the notes E, and G respectively. Play and say the note names aloud four times.

Climbing the Ladder

Beginning on the sixth string E (the lowest note) ascend by step to the note F on string four. Then return by step down to the note E. Play and say the note names aloud four times. By day three this should feel automatic.

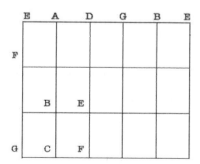

Hop and Skip

Beginning on the sixth string E open hop and skip up and down the following five tones: E, G, B, D, F. As you play these notes keep in mind these will be "space" notes. Play and say the note names aloud four times. By day three this should feel easy.

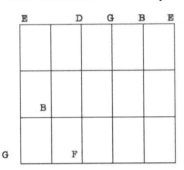

Beginning on the sixth string F (fret 1) hop and skip up and down the following four tones: F, A, C, E. As you play these notes keep in mind these will be "line" notes. Note the notes A and C are on string five. The other two tones, F and E, are on string 6 and 4 respectively. Play and say the note names aloud four times. By day three this should feel like a walk in the park.

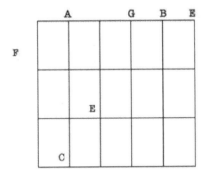

Because thirds are the building blocks of chords the first pattern of four (E-G-B-D) is an E minor seventh chord. The second pattern of four (G-B-D-F) is a G7. The third pattern (F-A-C-E) is a F major seventh chord.

Notes on the Sixth String

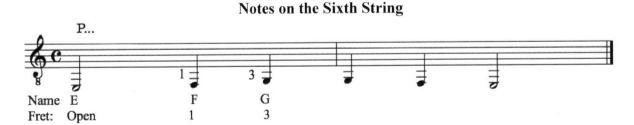

Read, say, and play the scale above four times. Notice E is below the third ledger line, and G is below the second ledger line.

Climbing the Ladder

The piece below is the same pattern of fingering and letter name notes you have learned by heart over the past two and a half days. With your eyes fixed on the page play and say note names aloud four times.

Climbing the Ladder

Hop and Skip

The piece below is the same pattern of fingering and letter name notes you have mastered over the past two and a half days. The first two bars as you can see are space notes, the third and fourth bars are line notes. The first two bars spell an E minor seventh and G seventh chord. The third and fourth bar spell a F major seventh chord; it could also spell an F chord (F-A-C) and an A minor chord (A-C-E). With your eyes fixed on the page play and say note names aloud four times.

Hop and Skip

Bass String Etude: If you can say it, you can play it!

This little study combines stepwise and sequential skips. Read the piece first saying the note names aloud. Attempt to say the note names at an even tempo. If this proves difficult, slow the tempo down. You may have to divide your practice into two-bar sub-phrase groupings. Reading the notes quickly is essential to attaining good sight-reading skills. By now, if you can say it, you can play it!

Bass String Etude

How Do You Do?

Now you have been properly introduced to the bass notes, try playing this tuneful pop tune. Don't be put off by the syncopated rhythms. Begin by saying the note names in proper time. Measure one may be more challenging because it hops around more. Get together with a classmate and play the song as a duet. One strums the chords, the other plays the tune.

How Do You Do?

Peter Jospeh Zisa

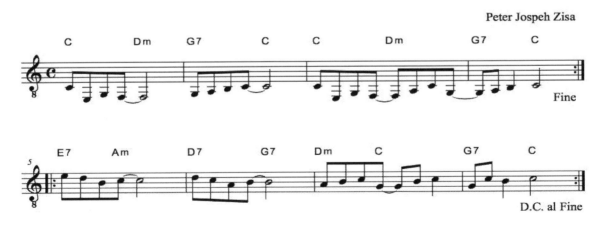

Iron Fly

The last tune is a rock-style piece in the spirit of the Black Sabbath and Iron Maiden. The most difficult part is the rhythm. You may want to practice the rhythm as a strum. In measure three and four strum the two-note chord downward with the thumb. The effect is a kind of double stop. The chords for the last two lines of the piece are Am (four beats) then F and G (two beats each). Note the bass melody in measure six and ten spell an F and G chord; this is also true in measure eight and twelve.

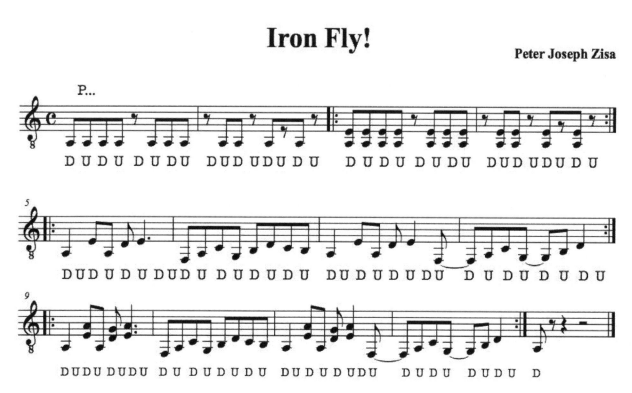

Lesson 17 Practice Calendar

Two Goals:
(1) Learn to read and play the fingered notes on the sixth string
(2) Master triple meter arpeggio pattern (p-i-m-a-m-i)

	Sunday	Monday	Tuesday	Wednesday	Thursday	Friday	Saturday
Scales							
Chords							
Arpeggio							
Strum							
New Songs							
Old Songs							

30 – 45 minutes

Scales: 2 minutes per day (Major scale)
(1) One octave at quarter note (one second) - four times. Major scale in the Key of C, G, D, A, E
(2) Shape melodic contour of scale. Begin *mp* and crescendo up to *F*, on the descent decrescendo to *mp*.
(3) Move right hand placement and experiment with tone color.
(4) Experiment with staccato (detached) effect. Strike string with one digit
   (e.g. "i") and immediately stop the resonating string with another (e.g. "m")

Chord changes - As applicable (3 minutes per day)
(1) Improve smoothness of difficult chord changes. Synchronized movement - fingers move and arrive at the same time.

Four Arpeggio Patterns: (10 minutes per day)
Two patterns a day: quarter note pace - four time minimum
Observe and correct position, follow through
Practice at four different dynamic levels: p, mp, mf, F

Strum Patterns - (10 minutes per day)
(1) Two patterns a day
(2) Accurate rhythm of the strum with index finger
(3) Strike correct number of strings
(4) Aim for a full down strum, and light up strung

Song repertoire - (20 minutes)
(1) **New Piece:** How Do You Do and/or Iron Fly
(2) **REVIEW Repertoire:** Quiet Desperation (Eleanor Rigby), 16-bar Blues, E-Z Does It (blues in E), Jamabalaya, Paperback Writer, Mary Had a Little Lamb, Aunt Rhody, Old Joe Clark, Heart and Soul, Bach in a Minuet, Miss You, Aura Lee (Love Me Tender), Hello My Baby, Five Foot Two, Ragged Time, Preludio Del Amore, Blowin' In the Wind, Rockin' the Boat, Piazza Di Spana, Traditional English Melody (House of the Rising Sun), How Do You Do?, Iron Fly!

Lesson 18: The Pentatonic Scale: A Scale for All Seasons and Times

Pentatonic Scale

The pentatonic scale is a five-tone scale. Pentatonic scales are found in music throughout world from the most ancient times to its popular use in contemporary music today. The universal use of the scale in world music has been the source of interest among musicologists and neuroscientists. In a science symposium "Notes & Neurons: In Search of the Common Chorus" Bobby McFerrin demonstrated the instinctive human connection we have with the scale (https://youtu.be/ne6tB2KiZuk).

Unlike the major and minor scales the pattern of intervals in a pentatonic scale is not uniform. Examine the five tones D – E – G – A – B. Depending on the starting tone of this scale, the series may have *minor* or *major quality*. For example, if the tonal center (key) is G the order of the notes would be G-A-B-D-E. Because the first *third* is major (G to B), it described as a *major* pentatonic scale. Change the starting tone to E, the order of the scale becomes E-G-A-B-D. This time the scale has a minor quality; this is because the first occurring third is a minor third (E to G).

Pentatonic Scale and Blues

While musicologists date earliest blues songs to the 19th century. The 12-bar AAB lyric form of the blues is found in early blues classics of Hart Wand's Dallas Blues (1912) and W.C. Handy's St. Louis Blues (1914). A distinguishing feature of 12-bar harmonic progression is it consists of solely three dominant-seventh chords: I7, IV7, V7.

‖: I7		(IV7)		I7		I7		
	IV7		IV7		I7		I7		
	V7		IV7		I7		V7	:‖

While the relationship of these chords remained tonic, sub-dominant, dominant respectively, this use of only dominant-seventh chords was harmonically unique. Traditionally the dominant-seventh chord is the strongest of the *dissonant* harmonies driving the listener to expect a nicely resolved tonic chord. The use of only dominant-seventh chords made early blues more dissonant than standard popular songs. Even the ending chord was not exempt from this treatment; most blues songs end on an unresolved dominant seventh (I7). Over the years, particularly in Jazz, ending on *unresolved* harmony took additional forms, such ending on a 9th, 11th, 13th, or a related harmony.

The melodies of the blues songs are derived from the pentatonic scale. Another difference of the use a pentatonic scale in the blues is presence of the *blue's note*. The *blues notes* are quarter tones; that is, notes that lie between semitones. Blues notes are literally *pulled out of tune*. There are two directional methods of playing these notes, the first is playing the written note and then pulling the string to raise the pitch a quarter tone. The second is to pull the string before striking the note, then afterwards releasing the note lowering down to standard pitch.

The musical meaning of blues notes and unresolved dominant-seventh chords is the perfect musical description of this racially oppressive times. Similarly, the popular appeal of the blues was powerful expression of feelings: from sadness to anger, forlorn loneliness to redemptive hope. The rebellious spirit of the blues served as the perfect musical transition to rhythm and blues (rock and roll). *Hard rock music* of the late 1960s and 1970s was a blues revival.

Blues and rock music make extensive improvisatory use of the pentatonic scale. The two pentatonic scale forms below are two of the five pentatonic-finger forms or patterns across the guitar fingerboard. The following patterns constitute two of the five patterns on the treble strings. Below the pattern are the key (tonal center) of the pattern.

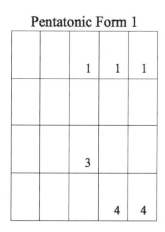

Pentatonic Form 1

Key	Position
E	I Open, IV
G	I Open, III
A	II, V
C	V, VIII

Pentatonic Form 2

Key	Position
E	IV, VII
G	VII, X
A	I Open, IX
C	I Open, III

The following are two standard blues keys to explore. Initially practice playing the scales up and down slowly. Change the position and compare the sound of the scale. Find a musical partner to team up with and exchange chord and improvisatory parts. Improvising a melody is spontaneously creating a melody. Begin with a simple repeated rhythmic idea. With each repetition of the rhythm change the melodic tones. In time you will learn to spontaneously create your own heartfelt melodies.

KEY OF C	‖: C7	I (F7*)	I C7	I C7	I	
	I G7	I G7	I F7	I F7	I	
	I G7	I F7	I C7	I G7	:‖ C7	‖

KEY OF G	‖: G7	I (C7)	I G7	I G7	I	
	I C7	I C7	I G7	I G7	I	
	I D7	I C7	I G7	I D7	:‖ G7	‖

KEY OF D	‖: D7	I (G7)	I D7	I D7	I	
	I A7	I A7	I D7	I D7	I	
	I A7	I G7	I D7	I A7	:‖ D7	‖

KEY OF A	‖: A7	I (D7)	I A7	I A7	I	
	I E7	I D7	I A7	I A7	I	
	I E7	I D7	I A7	I E7	:‖ A7	‖

KEY OF E	‖: E7	I (A7)	I E7	I E7	I	
	I A7	I A7	I E7	I E7	I	
	I B7	I A7	I E7	I B7	:‖ E7	‖

New chord:

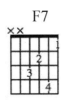

Lesson 18 Practice Calendar

Two Goals:

(1) Learn to read and play the fingered notes on the sixth string
(2) Master triple meter arpeggio pattern (p-i-m-a-m-i)

	Sunday	Monday	Tuesday	Wednesday	Thursday	Friday	Saturday
Scales							
Chords							
Arpeggio							
Strum							
New Songs							
Old Songs							

30 - 45 minutes

Scales: 2 minutes per day (Major scale)
    (1) One octave at quarter note (one second) - four times. Major scale in the Key of C, G, D, A, E
        Two pentatonic scale forms in four keys
    (2) Shape melodic contour of scale. Begin **mp** and crescendo up to **F,** on the descent
        decrescendo to **mp.**
    (3) Move right hand placement and experiment with tone color.
    (4) Experiment with staccato (detached) effect. Strike string with one digit (e.g. "i")
        and immediately stop the resonating string with another (e.g. "m")

Chord changes - As applicable (3 minutes per day)
    Improve smoothness of difficult chord changes. Synchronized movement - fingers move and arrive at the same time.

Four Arpeggio Patterns: (10 minutes per day)
Two patterns a day: quarter note pace - four time minimum
Observe and correct position, follow through
 Practice at four different dynamic levels: p, mp, mf, F

Strum Patterns - (10 minutes per day)
    (1) Two patterns a day
    (2) Accurate rhythm of the strum with index finger
    (3) Strike correct number of strings
    (4) Aim for a full down strum, and light up strung

Song repertoire - (20 minutes)
    (1) **New Piece:** 12-Bar Blues in Five Keys
    (2) **REVIEW Repertoire:** Blowin' In the Wind, Rockin' the Boat, Piazza Di Spana,
        Traditional English Melody (House of the Rising Sun), How Do You Do?, Iron Fly!

Lesson 19: Tablature: Yesterday, Today, and…

Thus far you have learned to read music using standard notation. This lesson focuses on the guitar's first and most enduring form of notation: tablature. There are advantages and limitations with tablature. It will be helpful for you to learn how to read guitar tablature. Some guitar music is easier to read and play in tablature; this particularly true when the guitar music uses altered tuning.

History of Guitar Notation

During the 15th and 16th century the guitar was a four-course instrument. The tuning of the four-string guitar is the same as it commonly is today. There does not appear to be any time signature. The notation uses letters to denote the fingered notes. The letter *a* is an open string; letter b, c, and d represent the first, second, and third fret respectively. The highest string (string 1) is the top line; the lowest line is the fourth string. How would you decipher the rhythmic symbols above the notes? How many beats per measure can you infer? What modern equivalent would the one-line flag and two-line flag notes be?

Listen to the piece "La Seraphine" (https://youtu.be/T54nhka_hIo) by French Renaissance guitar composer **Guillaume de Morlaye** (c.1510–c.1558). *Seraphine* is a girl's name; in Hebrew it means "burning fire". You will notice Jocelyn Nelson's performance of the piece has a lot of gentle strumming. This was characteristic of early guitar music; in contrast, the music of the plucked lute and vihuela often had complex the polyphonic (many-voiced) textures. What else about this 16th century piece stands out to you?

The renaissance lute music by Italian composer Francesco da Milano (1497-1543) was a six-course instrument. Five of the courses were doubled strings (like today's 12-string guitar). Italian and Spanish tablature example used numbers instead of letters to designate the fret position of the notes. The bottom line represents the first string and the top line the sixth. The tuning of the lute and Spanish vihuela were tuned similar to the guitar. One difference is the third string was tuned to F-sharp. The meter is not indicated in the example below, however, it is easy to read and infer the time values of the notes. Can you read the first eight measure of the top strings below? Remember to tune your third string down to F-sharp!

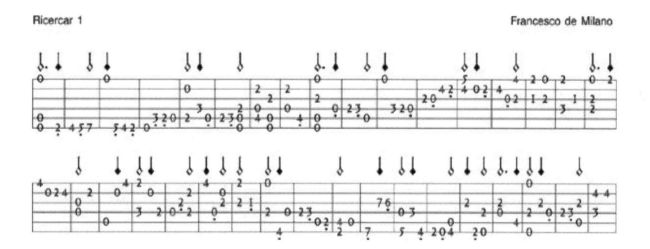

In the baroque period (1600 – 1750) the guitar became a five-course instrument. The piece below by Count Ludovico Roncalli (1654-1713) is a Gavotte from one of the nine suites he composed for guitar. Like Vivaldi, Roncalli was an ordained priest and educated in civil and canon (church) law. The gavotte is a lively peasant "kissing" dance. It was popular in England and France. The time signature is marked with a C, common time. The rhythm of the dance is notated above the numbered notation. The bottom line is the first string and the top line the fifth string. Try playing the melody of the A section, the first four bars.

What is the clear advantages of tablature notation? What are the ambiguities and shortcomings of this notational system? What are the advantages of standard notation?

Tablature Today

Today's tablature system is more standardized. Commonly the lowest line in the six-line system represents the sixth string, and the top line the first. The placement of the tones is specified with numbers. The following piece, *Driftwood,* is written in both tablature and standard notation. This practice is commonly found in popular guitar arrangements today. While the tablature system shows the placement of the notes on the fingerboard, the fingering of the notes is indicated above in the standard notation. Read through the tablature and compare to the written notation above.

Driftwood

Reading Tablature

Peter Joseph Zisa

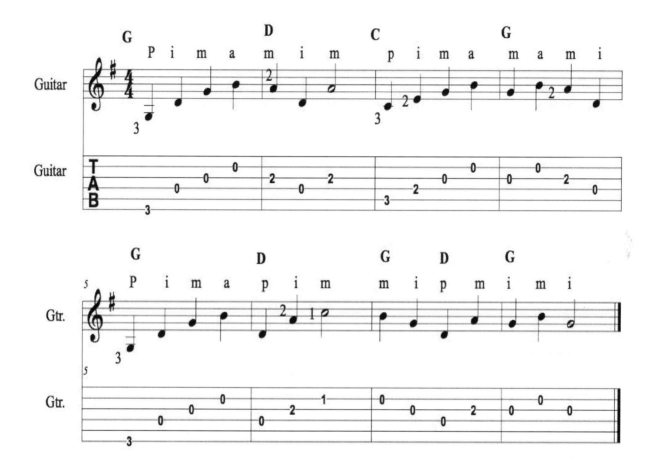

The following piece uses "Travis-picking" commonly found Delta Blues style.

Lesson 19 Practice Calendar

Two Goals:

(1) Learn to read and play tablature
(2) "Travis-picking" used in Delta Blues style

	Sunday	Monday	Tuesday	Wednesday	Thursday	Friday	Saturday
Scales							
Chords							
Arpeggio							
Strum							
New Songs							
Old Songs							

30 - 45 minutes

Scales: 2 minutes per day (Major scale)
(1) One octave at quarter note (one second) - four times. Major scale in the Key of C, G, D, A, E
(2) Two pentatonic scale forms in four keys
(3) Shape melodic contour of scale. Begin **mp** and crescendo up to **F**, on the descent decrescendo to **mp.**
(4) Move right hand placement and experiment with tone color.
(5) Experiment with staccato (detached) effect. Strike string with one digit (e.g. "i") and immediately stop the resonating string with another (e.g. "m")

Chord changes - As applicable (3 minutes per day)
Improve smoothness of difficult chord changes. Synchronized movement - fingers move and arrive at the same time.

Four Arpeggio Patterns: (10 minutes per day)
Two patterns a day: quarter note pace - four time minimum
Observe and correct position, follow through
Practice at four different dynamic levels: p, mp, mf, F

Strum Patterns - (10 minutes per day)
(1) Two patterns a day
(2) Accurate rhythm of the strum with index finger
(3) Strike correct number of strings
(4) Aim for a full down strum, and light up strung

Song repertoire - (20 minutes)
(1) **New Pieces:** Driftwood & Mississippi Blues
(2) **REVIEW Repertoire:** Blowin' In the Wind, Rockin' the Boat, Piazza Di Spana, Traditional English Melody (House of the Rising Sun), How Do You Do?, Iron Fly!

Lesson 20: Alternative Tunings

The *Professional Competencies* document of the American Music Therapy Association (2013) require music therapist to increase their musical skills so they can play traditional, folk, and popular songs from different eras (Leist, 2015). Because these music genres include also alternative tunings for the guitar, the listed 2013 skill requirements also require music therapists to demonstrate competency using standard tuning and alternative tunings (Leist, 2015). This lesson introduces you to two of the most common alternative tunings; they are Drop D tuning and DADGAD (Celtic) tuning.

Drop-D Tuning

The range of standard tuning of the guitar from the open sixth string to the open first is two octaves. The interval relationship from string to string, with the exception of the third and second string, is a perfect fourth. An alternative tuning represents a different range of notes across the span of six strings and a different interval relationship from string to string. Drop-D tuning lowers the sixth string a whole step, from E to D.

Drop-D tuning is commonly used for songs in the key of D (major and minor). The sixth string D adds fullness to the D chord. One of the drawbacks of the Drop-D tuning is playing the G (IV) chord in root position. The position of the low G in Drop-D is on the fifth fret of the sixth string. Options to avoid this complication include using the low D note as a pedal tone (a sustained or repeated tone); a G chord may then be played (as a second-inversion chord) with the D as the bass, as shown below.

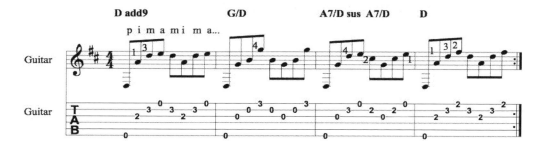

The added overtones provided by low-D on the string six adds warmth and fullness to the harmonic texture. A tonic pedal tone also creates static tension. In contrast, the use of a dominant pedal tone creates greater harmonic tension (as shown below).

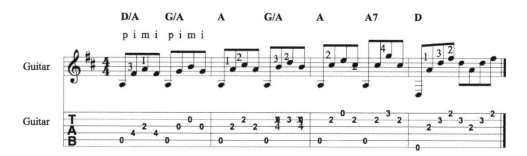

Jasmine

Jasmine is an example of Drop-D tuning. The first four bars of the piece begin with a four-chord progression: D, D/F# (first inversion D chord), G, and A7. The right-hand fingering of each four-note arpeggio uses the right-hand thumb twice to play the sixth and fourth string and skipping the fifth string. The chord changes are relatively simple and straightforward. The only potential problem is the position of the left hand in playing the first two bars. It is important to square off the left-hand position when transitioning from the D to the D/F# chord. The third chord simply moves up a fret to position three, followed by the hand shifting back to first position for the familiar A7 fourth chord.

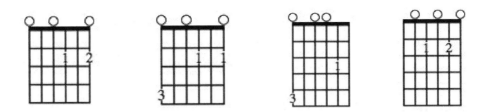

The second line of the piece is nearly identical to the first four bars. The chord progression of contrasting third line begins with a simple E minor. The last four bars of the piece use similar chords to the second half of the first phrase.

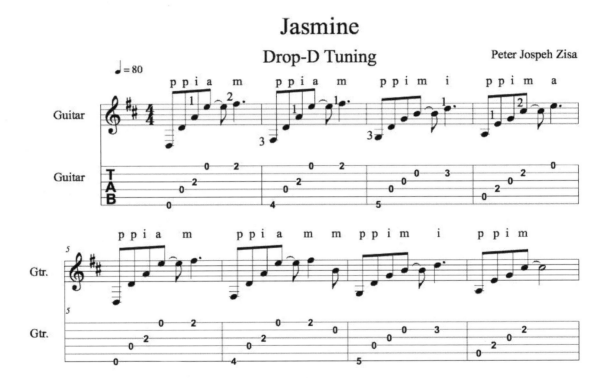

DADGAD Tuning Its History and Use

The origin of DADGAD tuning is unclear. In the early 1960s Davey Graham (1940 – 2008), a British folk guitarist, is credited for generated interest in his new style fingerstyle (finger picking). One element for his stylistic uniqueness was his incorporation of an alternative tuning for the guitar called DADGAD. Graham however did not invent DADGAD. According to popular folklore, Graham discovered the tuning while on tour in Morocco. Graham's popular song "She Moves through the Fair - https://www.youtube.com/watch?v=hvpTVn_Ltzc

The tuning allows for an interesting use of open drone tones, which is common in Scottish and Irish bagpipe music. It is for this reason this tuning is described as Celtic tuning. It is worth noting the origin of bagpipes is Persian. The bagpipes, like the oud (lute), was introduced to Europe by the Moors. Eventually the bagpipes were introduced to Scotland and Ireland where the instrument was adopted.

DADGAD tuning has a modal quality. The sonority of the open strings is a D chord (no third) with "G", the open third string, as a suspended fourth. The resulting "harmony" is neither major or minor. In the 1960s, inspired by Davey Graham, folk and rock guitarists melodically and harmonically explored the nuances of the scale.

Jimmy Page described DADGAD as his "CIA" (Celtic, Indian, and Arabic) tuning. A great example of this mixture can be heard in Page's improvisational work using this scale may be heard https://www.youtube.com/watch?v=n4WJO1dfM6o . Page's most famous CIA composition is Kashmir (https://youtu.be/9vbeilE0UrQ).

DADGAD Tuning

The name DADGAD refers to the alternative tuning of the open strings. Unlike the standard tuning of the guitar (**EADGBE**), DADGAD lowers the open sixth, second, and first string a whole step. As mentioned, with the exception of the third string, the tuning is made of two notes: D and A.

```
D
A
G
D
A
D
```

Sunset

DADgad Tuning

Peter Joseph Zisa

Lesson 20 Practice Calendar

Two Goals:

(1) Learn to read and play in Drop-D Tuning.
(2) Learn to read and play in DADGAD Tuning.

	Sunday	Monday	Tuesday	Wednesday	Thursday	Friday	Saturday
Scales							
Chords							
Arpeggio							
Strum							
New Songs							
Old Songs							

30 - 45 minutes

Scales: 2 minutes per day (Major scale)
(1) One octave at quarter note (one second) - four times. Major scale in the Key of C, G, D, A, E
Two pentatonic scale forms in four keys
(2) Shape melodic contour of scale. Begin **mp** and crescendo up to **F**, on the descent decrescendo to **mp.**
(3) Move right hand placement and experiment with tone color.
(4) Experiment with staccato (detached) effect. Strike string with one digit (e.g. "i") and immediately stop the resonating string with another (e.g. "m")

Chord changes - As applicable (3 minutes per day)
Improve smoothness of difficult chord changes. Synchronized movement - fingers move and arrive at the same time.

Four Arpeggio Patterns: (10 minutes per day)
    a. Two patterns a day: quarter note pace - four time minimum
    b. Observe and correct position, follow through
    c. Practice at four different dynamic levels: p, mp, mf, F

Strum Patterns - (10 minutes per day)
(1) Two patterns a day
(2) Accurate rhythm of the strum with index finger
(3) Strike correct number of strings
(4) Aim for a full down strum, and light up strung

Song repertoire - (20 minutes)
(1) **New Pieces:** Jasmine (Drop D) and Sunset (DADGAD)
(2) **REVIEW Repertoire:** Blowin' In the Wind, Rockin' the Boat, Piazza Di Spana, Traditional English Melody (House of the Rising Sun), How Do You Do?, Iron Fly!

Summary Review

This concluding portion of your **how to** guide to play is intended to be a helpful reference section. This section consolidates much of the material of the book. It is divided into five sections: scale forms, strumming patterns, arpeggiated patterns, chord fingerings and chord progressions (in five keys).

Scales:

Ascending Chromatic Scale

E 0	A 0	D 0	G 0	B 0	E 0
			G#	C	F
			A	C#	F#
			A#	D	G
			D#		

Descending Chromatic Scale

E 0	A 0	D 0	G 0	B 0	E 0
			A flat	C	F
			A	D flat	G flat
			B flat	D	G
			E flat		

Five Keys

Key	Position
C	5
G*	1
D	7
A	2
E	9

One Octave Major-Scale Form

			1	1	1
				2	
			3		3
				4	4

Practice Improv to tonic and dominant-seventh progression ‖: I | V7 | V7 | I :‖

*The G major scale in position one contains open strings (see below).

G major Scale

145

Pentatonic Scale

The melodies of the blues are primarily pentatonic. "Blue notes" are tones are quarter tones; that is, notes that lie between semitones. There are five pentatonic-finger patterns across the guitar fingerboard. The following patterns constitute two of the five patterns on the treble strings. Below each pattern are the key (tonal center) and corresponding finger position of the pattern.

Pentatonic Form 1		Pentatonic Form 2	
(diagram showing fingering: 1,1,1 / 3 / 4,4)		(diagram showing fingering: 1,1 / 2 / 3 / 4,4)	

Key	Position
E	I Open, IV
G	I Open, III
A	II, V
C	V, VIII

Key	Position
E	IV, VII
G	VII, X
A	I Open, IX
C	I Open, III

12-Bar Blues Progression

‖: I7 | (IV7) | I7 | I7 |
| IV7 | IV7 | I7 | I7 |
| V7 | IV7 | I7 | V7   :‖

Chord Strumming

Strumming is rhythmically conceived harmony. The counting of the strums below are centered on the dance characteristic of rhythm. Synchronize the down and upward movement of the hand with the tapping movement of your foot and swaying movement your body.

Rhythm Strum Patterns in Simple Quadruple Meter
Strumming rhythms provides a both rhythmic and a harmonic accompaniment to singing and music making. Choosing a rhythmic strum pattern effects the emotional and musical energy you hope to generate. Choices may be range from gentle half note strums to spirited syncopated rhythms. Your decision may be stylistic, pedagogic, or musical. A stylistic strum reflects the rhythm characteristic of the music; e.g., how a rumba rhythmic is different than a tango or a bossa-nova. The following patterns provide a range of choices, from steady and even to syncopated and spirited.

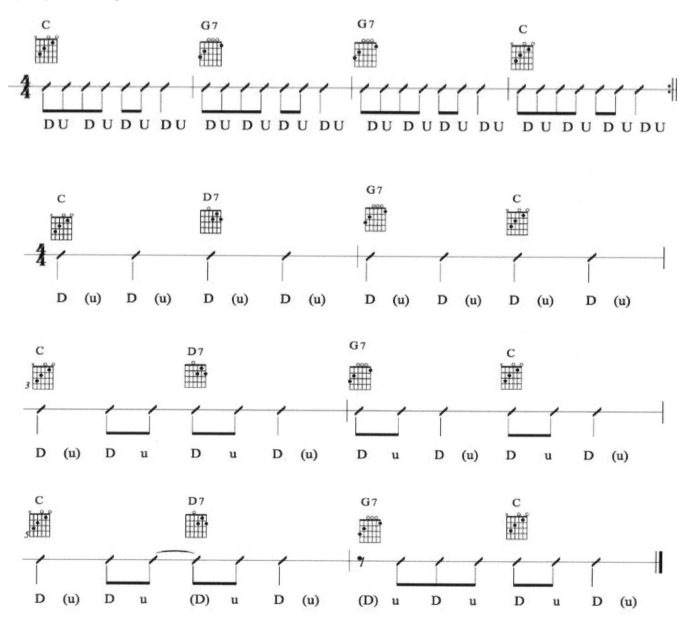

Rhythm Strum Patterns in Simple Quadruple Meter

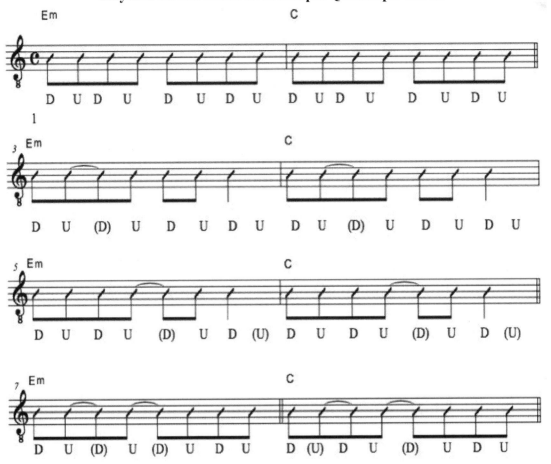

This system has two represented chords per measure, each of which receives two beats. The initial down strum of each harmonic change should generally include the full range of chord tones..

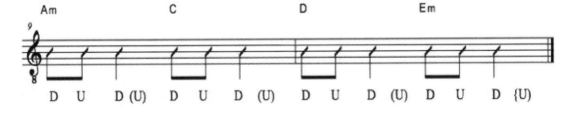

Rhythm Strum Patterns in Simple Triple Meter

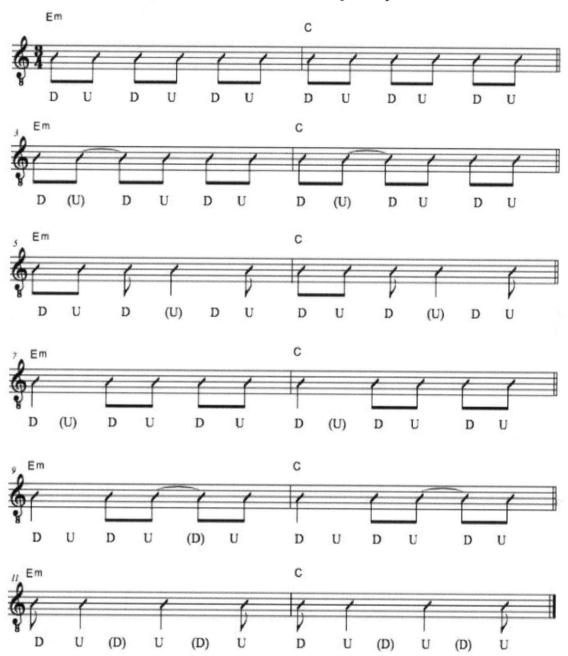

Arpeggio Forms in Simple Quadruple Meter

The following arpeggio summative material is presented in the form of a four-chord progression (see below). The thumb (p) is assigned the three bass strings. The index (i), middle (m), and ring (a) finger of the right hand are assigned the third, second, and first string respectively. The bass notes may all be played rest stroke (apoyando). Use free stroke (tirando) for i, m. a.

Arpeggio Forms in Simple Triple Meter

Chords & Chord Progression

The following chords section is arranged as a set common chord progressions. Learning sets of chord progressions is a superior pedagogic approach to developing a music therapy repertoire list because for each progression represents scores of songs. Each progression is presented in five keys; C, G, D, A, and E. A few song name examples are identified for each progression.

I V7 Chord Progressions in Five Keys
Tom Dooley, Down by the Riverside, Jambalaya, Give Peace A Chance

	I	V7	V7	I
C major	C	G7	G7	C
G major	G	D7	D7	G
D major	D	A7	A7	D
A major	A	E7	E7	A
E major	E	B7	B7	E

This progression matches nicely for two guitars, one playing chords the another playing one octave major scale. ‖: I | V7 | V7 | I :‖

I - ii - V7 - I Chord Progressions in Five Keys
Satin Doll, Take the A Train, Misty
Summertime, Autumn Leaves, Blue Bossa, Honeysuckle Rose,

	I	ii	V7	I
C major	C	Dm	G7	C
G major	G	Am7	D7	G
D major	D	Em	A7	D
A major	A	Bm7	E7	A
E major	E	F#m7	B7	E

I - vi - ii - V7 - I Chord Progressions in Five Keys
Used in jazz, R&B, pop, rock, and country
Blue Moon, Beyond the Sea, Crocodile Rock, Every Breath You Take, Give a Little Lo

	I	**vi**	**ii**	**V7**
C major	C	Am7	Dm	G7
G major	G	Em	Am7	D7
D major	D	Bm7	Em	A7
A major	A	F#m7	Bm7	E7
E major	E	C#m7	F#m7	B7

I - VI7 - II7 - V7 - I Chord Progressions in Five Keys
Toot Toot Tootsie, Hello My Baby, Five Foot Two

	I	VI7	II7	V7	I
C major	C	A7	D7	G7	C
G major	G	E7	A7	D7	G
D major	D	B7	E7	A7	D
A major	A	F#7	B7	E7	A
E major	E	C#7	F#7	B7	E

I - V - IV - I Chord Progressions in Five Keys
Bad Moon Rising, Sweet Caroline, Key to the Highway

	I	V	IV	I
C major	C	G	F	C
G major	G	D	C	G
D major	D	G	A	D
A major	A	E	D	A
E major	E	B7	A	E

I - IV - V7 - I Chord Progressions in Five Keys
La Bamba, Twist and Shout, Stir It Up, Fulson Prison Blues

	I	IV	V7	I
C major	C	F	G7	C
G major	G	C	D	G
D major	D	G	A	D
A major	A	D	E7	A
E major	E	A	B7	E

i - iv - V7 - i Chord Progressions in Three Minor Keys
Anniversary Song, Tarantella, Sunrise Sunset

	i	iv	V7	i
E minor	Em	Am	B7	Em
A minor	Am	Dm	E7	Am
D minor	Dm	Gm	A7	Dm

References

Aigen, K. (2001). Popular music styles in Nordoff-Robbins music therapy. Gilsum, NH: Barcelona Publishers.

Aigen, K. (2001). Playin' in the band: A qualitative study of popular music styles as clinical improvisation. New York, NY: Nordoff-Robbins Center for Music Therapy, New York University.

Burnstein, S, and Powell, B. (2016, May 18). Teaching Guitar through Popular Music Education. National Association for Music Education. Retrieved from https://nafme.org/teaching-guitar-popular-music-education/

Fries, P., 2005. A mechanism for cognitive dynamics: neuronal communication through neuronal coherence. Trends Cogn. Sci. 9 (10), 474-480. http://dx.doi.org/10.1016/j.tics.2005.08.011.

Haneishi, E. (2005). Juliette alvin: Her legacy for music therapy in japan. *Journal of Music Therapy, 42(4),* 273-95. Retrieved from http://search.proquest.com/docview/223558415?accountid=35812

Hurley, K. R. (2008). *Validating music therapy and its effectiveness in treating brain disorders: The role of emotions in music and in therapy* (Order No. 1461305). Retrieved from http://search.proquest.com/docview/304568123?accountid=35812

Leist, Christine P,PhD., M.T.-B.C. (2015). A guide to selected alternate guitar tunings for music therapists. *Music Therapy Perspectives, 33*(1), 71-75. doi:http://dx.doi.org/10.1093/mtp/miu041

James, J. (1993). The music of the spheres. New York, NY: Copernicus.

Melloni, L., Molina, C., Pena, M., Torres, D., Singer, W., Rodriguez, E., 2007. Synchronization of neural activity across cortical areas correlates with conscious perception. J. Neurosci. 27 (11), 2858-2865. http://dx.doi.org/10.1523/ jneurosci.4623-06.2007.

Music and Mood - https://www.ideals.illinois.edu/bitstream/handle/2142/14956/Music%26Mood-final.pdf?sequence=2

Music and Emotion - http://csml.som.ohio-state.edu/Music829D/music829D.bibliography.html#Music%20and%20Emotion%20-%20Philosophical

Panksepp, J., Biven, L. (2012). The archaeology of mind: Neuroevolutionary origins of human emotions. New York, NY: Norton Publishing.

Sievers, B., Polansky, L., Casey, M., & Wheatley, T. (2013). Music and movement share a dynamic structure that supports universal expressions of emotion. *Proceedings of the National Academy of Sciences of the United States of America, 110(1),* 70–75. http://doi.org/10.1073/pnas.1209023110

John B - Sails

| D | D^{sus} (beat 4) | | A | A^{sus} | | D | D^{sus} |

| G | G^{sus} (beat 4) | | D | | A | | D | |